forget
me not

Health Problems in Older People

people experience mental health problems such as nd depression.

:ation and Initial Responses ces

d information and advice at an early stage, but GPs difficulty in providing appropriate assistance.

to Help People at Home

le with mental health problems need access to a range including home care, outpatient clinics, respite care and

l and Residential Provision

issions to hospital might be avoided, and the quality roved, if mental health professionals provided better residential and nursing homes.

nation between Services

Health and social services need to share information with each other and to co-ordinate with GPs and other service providers.

6  Developing a Comprehensive Strategy

Commissioners have a key role in drawing together all of the elements of a comprehensive service.

Contents

© Audit Commission 2000

First published in January 2000 by the Audit Commission for Local Authorities
and the National Health Service in England and Wales, 1 Vincent Square,
London SW1P 2PN

Printed in the UK for the Audit Commission by Holbrooks Printers Ltd,
Portsmouth

ISBN 1 86240 203 5

Photographs: Paul Baldesare/Photofusion (p35), Debbie Humphrey/Photofusion
(64), David Mansell (cover, pp3, 8, 50, 60, 74, 83, 96) with thanks to the
Petersfield Centre, Essex, Joanne O'Brien/Format (p6), Roy Peters/Alzheimer's
Disease Society (p38), Hilary Shedel (p20).

Preface

The Audit Commission oversees the external audit of local authorities and the National Health Service (NHS) in England and Wales. As part of this function, the Commission is required to undertake studies to enable it to make recommendations for improving the economy, efficiency and effectiveness of services provided by these bodies.

Over the last 18 months, the Commission has been reviewing services for older people with mental health problems provided by the public sector, and its findings are set out in this report. Cross-cutting audits of these services, covering health and social care, will take place throughout England and Wales during 2000 and 2001. For the first time, auditors have been appointed to work across the agencies within local areas.

This is the first in a series of reports with a common theme of promoting independence for older people. Other reports in this series will look at rehabilitation and remedial services, disability equipment and charging arrangements for home care by local authorities. It follows previous reports *Finding A Place*, in 1994, which looked at mental health services for younger adults, and *The Coming of Age*, in 1997, which reviewed the health and social care for older people.

The study on which this report is based was carried out by Judy Renshaw and Peter Scurfield, under the direction of David Browning. Most of the data preparation and analysis was carried out by Louise Cloke, Justin Caldwell and Tom Dixon. Particular thanks go to Dr Martin Orrell, who was the professional advisor to the study. Thanks also go to our external advisory group, listed at Appendix 1; and to Ruth Cutts who has played a major part in shaping the audit.

3

Introduction

1. More and more people are living on to old age. The greatest rise in the next ten years (14 per cent) will be among those over 80, to 2.3 million (Ref. 1). But growing numbers of older people mean growing mental health problems. Although people over 65 represent only 16 per cent of the population, they use a disproportionate percentage of both physical and mental health care. 'Old' older people experience the most mental health problems. One-quarter of those over 85 develop dementia, and between 10 and 16 per cent of those over 65 develop clinical depression. Other mental health problems, such as anxiety and phobias, are at least as common as they are in younger people. In addition, people who developed severe and enduring mental health problems such as schizophrenia when young are now growing older.

The growing attention given to mental health care for older people

2. Public concern about being able to care for the growing number of older people, as well as concern about mental health generally, has led to renewed interest in this area. The recent failures of some services to provide satisfactory mental health care for younger people, such as the Christopher Clunis case (Ref. 2), have led to inquiries and public debate.

3. Mental health care has remained a key area for policy since it was identified in the last Government's *Health of the Nation* strategy. A key area handbook on the mental health of older people (Ref. 3) provided a statement of the range of services that would be useful in local areas and the way in which parts of the network should link together. Joint working between agencies, with shared aims and values, is a central feature of such a service. The Royal Commission on Long Term Care has made a series of recommendations on the funding of care for older people, in an attempt to make the system fairer for users and carers, while keeping it affordable (Ref. 4).

4. The Royal Colleges of Psychiatrists and Physicians issued a joint statement on specialist services for this group (Ref. 5). This recommended the development of a national framework, against which commissioners and the public could judge local practice and standards. It also recommended that service agreements between commissioners and providers should be explicit about the quality standards required, and that partnership working is developed between providing agencies.

5. The Government is giving mental health for older people priority. It has issued guidance for promoting 'Better Services for Vulnerable People' (Ref. 6), which requires health and local authorities in England, in partnership with NHS trusts, to agree local joint investment plans (JIPs). The plans are to include a joint analysis of:

- population need;
- current resources;
- current activity and expenditure; and
- agreed service outcomes.

One-quarter of those over 85 develop dementia, and between 10 and 16 per cent of those over 65 develop clinical depression

JIPs have to identify detailed priorities and specific targets covering the next three years. The first JIPs for older people, which must include older people with mental illness, were required by April 1999 and are to be updated annually. 'Better Services for Vulnerable People' does not apply in Wales, and there is no formal requirement for health and local authorities to submit JIPs, but the guidance on service priorities continues to stress the importance of multi-agency planning and there is a high expectation that health authorities and local authorities will work together. The development of primary care groups and trusts in England and local health groups in Wales is strengthening the role of GPs and primary care professionals in commissioning health services. The local health groups in Wales are coterminous with unitary local authorities, which should help the agencies to work together.

6. Arrangements that allow closer working are also being strengthened following the consultation papers *Partnership in Action* (Ref. 7) in England and *Partnership for Improvement* (Ref. 8) in Wales. These set out the basis for shared health and social services arrangements, including the relaxation of rules about funding for health and social care. Until now health and social services agencies have been unable to pool their resources to any significant extent, hindering the development of integrated services. The NHS Act 1999 (Ref. 9) now allows pooled funds, 'lead commissioning' and integrated provision. This should enable greater flexibility in the management and staffing of mental health services for older people, with resources from either body used in the most appropriate way to suit local circumstances.

7. In 2000 a National Service Framework is due to be published, setting out new standards for the care of older people. Mental health has been identified as a priority area. The framework is intended to improve quality and to decrease inequities in services across the country.

8. The Carers' Recognition and Service Act 1995 (Ref. 10) gives carers the right to an independent assessment of their needs, as distinct from the needs of the person they are caring for, if their dependant has a right to a community care assessment. It does not, however, give them any rights to services to meet the needs identified.

The study of mental health services for older people

9. In the light of the reconfiguration of commissioning and provision, it is increasingly important that the elements of an effective service are in place, and that cross-agency working is strengthened rather than disrupted. To this end, the Audit Commission is supporting such initiatives with a programme of studies and audits throughout 2000 and 2001 around the theme of promoting independence for older people. This report on mental health services for older people is the first in this programme.

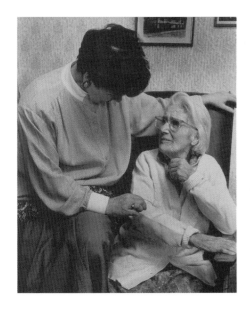

10. *Forget Me Not* is concerned with the services providing care to people with mental health problems over the age of 65. The two largest groups are those with dementia and those with depression. Care for people under 65 with dementia is also included here, as it usually falls within the remit of these services. The report covers services provided by NHS trusts, health authorities and social services departments, including some of the residential and nursing home care that they purchase. It does not address in detail the circumstances of those who are not in touch with specialist services.

11. The study was carried out in twelve areas of England and Wales, usually health authority areas, with visits to health trusts, health authorities, local authority social services and independent provider agencies. In addition to interviewing staff at all levels, and users and carers, a range of instruments was used to collect data and to provide comparative information [BOX A]. The study found a wide variation in practice, in the kinds of resources that were available, how effectively the agencies worked together, what carers felt about their local services and how commissioners were able to shape the pattern of provision. Older people and their carers have often not received the help they need, when they need it. The study describes how health and social care agencies need to work together to provide:

- help and advice when problems first arise;

- specialist services, especially to people in their own homes;

- co-ordination between the agencies and professions; and

- a comprehensive strategy to ensure all of the components are in place.

12. Chapter 1 gives an introduction to the kinds of mental health problems experienced by older people and the services available to help them. In Chapter 2 the ways in which people gain access to specialist services are explored. GPs are the gateway for most people, but social services, carers' groups and other voluntary organisations can provide other options, as well as providing essential support and information. Chapter 3 describes the range of services available to help people in their own homes, including home-based care, day and outpatient provision and respite care. It also compares the performance of services in different areas. Chapter 4 examines residential and hospital services across the range of providing agencies for those who are unable to stay at home. In Chapter 5 communication and co-ordination between the agencies are explored. These are essential if users are to receive comprehensive care that meets their needs. In Chapter 6 the role of strategic planning and commissioning, in bringing together the elements of provision examined in the previous chapters and evaluating the quality of services, is considered.

13. Throughout 2000 and 2001 local audits of services for older people with mental health problems will take place across health and social services agencies within JIP areas in England and local health groups in

Wales. For the first time, auditors are being appointed specifically to look at progress on these issues across agencies. They will focus on the issues highlighted in this report – in particular, the ways in which the communication and co-ordination between agencies could be improved. This should help with developing joint plans for services for older people.

BOX A

The instruments used in the study

- **Resource mapping:** this was a summary of all the resources available for home-based care, day and outpatient provision, residential/inpatient care and other services from both health and social services in 1997/98, together with their costs and levels of activity.

- **Individual case information (ICI):** this gathered brief details of a sample of users on the caseloads of community staff and those receiving services such as day care, hospital and residential care. It included a measure of dependency, using the behaviour rating scale of the Clifton Assessment Procedures for the Elderly (CAPE). This scale has been widely used in services for older people and has been found to be easy to use, as well as to be satisfactory for measuring reliability and validity (Refs. 11 and 12).

- **Case file analysis:** this covered ten or more individuals who had been referred to specialist mental health services twelve months earlier, and involved examining the files held on them by the different agencies. It looked at the assessments carried out, the different professions and agencies involved, the extent of users' and carers' involvement and the actions taken following the assessments.

- **GP survey:** this gauged GPs' attitudes to the identification of dementia and depression, the training and support they received and their views on local services. It was based on a previous survey undertaken by the University of Kent at Canterbury (Ref.13).

- **Carers' survey:** this covered 300 carers of individuals with dementia in the local area. Some were approached through the local statutory services and others through the Alzheimer's Disease Society (ADS). The survey asked about their experiences of seeking and receiving help and their views on local services.

- **Local data summary:** this summarised relevant activity data from local information systems, including re-admissions to hospital following discharge and the activity of local community mental health teams.

- **Checklist:** this was a checklist of 60 questions about the operation of local services. It was completed by the study team on the basis of interviews with staff, a review of documentation and the use of the different instruments listed above.

1

Mental Health Problems in Older People

Dementia is common in older people and is the result of physical changes in the brain that can lead to confusion and behaviour problems. Depression is also common in older people. Services to help them can be provided by health or social services, or other bodies such as voluntary organisations. Older people with mental health problems and their carers need a flexible range of services to enable them to remain at home for as long as possible.

Types of mental health problems

Dementia

14. Dementia refers to a cluster of signs and symptoms of intellectual and cognitive functioning being disrupted, usually in a progressive way that cannot be reversed. They are also called organic mental health problems, as they are linked to major physical changes in the brain. Four levels or stages have been described (Ref. 14), although they merge into each other and individuals will vary in the way in which their condition progresses.

- **Minimal:** where the person has some difficulty in recalling recent events and may mislay or lose things.

- **Mild:** where the person's recent memory is very poor and they are sometimes confused or disorientated.

- **Moderate:** where the person is usually disorientated in time and place, and has difficulty in reasoning or understanding. Sometimes they are incontinent and their emotional control deteriorates.

- **Severe:** where the person is totally disorientated, unable to communicate in normal speech, may fail to recognise close relatives, and is incontinent and completely dependent on others for personal care. Some people with severe dementia may be aggressive or violent to others. As the dementia progresses, the person can become immobile and totally physically dependent.

15. There are also different levels of 'need for care', depending on how long an individual can remain alone or independent without needing help (Ref. 15):

- **Independent:** care not needed.

- **Long interval:** care needed at least once a week.

- **Short interval:** care needed at least once daily.

- **Critical interval:** care or supervision needed continually or at brief irregular intervals each day.

Individual needs tend to vary from time to time, so services need to be flexible.

Types of dementia

16. Alzheimer's Disease is the most common form of dementia, and accounts for around 50–60 per cent of cases (Ref. 16). Those experiencing an early onset of the disease tend to progress more rapidly and are more likely to have a genetic cause for their illness. People with Down's syndrome, for example, are more likely to develop Alzheimer's Disease (Refs. 17 and 18) – up to 40 per cent in those over 50 (Ref. 19). There is some evidence that people who have been educated to a higher level are less likely to experience Alzheimer's Disease and its onset might be delayed (Ref. 20).

*In the early stages,
both they and their
close relatives may be
distressed and uncertain
about what might
be wrong*

17. Vascular dementia is the next most common form, and accounts for around 20 per cent of cases (Ref. 21). It is the result of damage to small areas of the brain, sometimes following a stroke. The loss of functioning depends on which parts of the brain have been affected. The risk factors are similar to those for heart disease, so stopping smoking, a suitable diet, exercise and aspirin may help to prevent it. Some people have mixed Alzheimer's and vascular dementia.

18. Dementia with Lewy Bodies has become recognised as a common form since the early 1980s, although it is difficult to identify accurately. Some people experience visual hallucinations and parkinsonism, making it distinctly identifiable (Ref. 22). In addition, some kinds of dementia are due to other causes, such as AIDS, Creutzfeldt Jakob Disease, Huntington's Disease and Pick's Disease. Many of those with severe dementia, especially those over 85, have a combination of mental and physical problems.

19. People with some kinds of dementia have lower than normal levels of the neural transmitter acetyl choline in the brain. This has led to the development of a number of new drugs that increase the amount of this chemical, by reducing enzyme activity, for example. They do not redress the damage to the brain cells, but may ameliorate the effects for a limited period of time.

Effects of dementia

20. People with dementia and their carers mainly need help in dealing with its social consequences. In the early stages, both they and their close relatives may be distressed and uncertain about what might be wrong. It is not unusual for them to withdraw from their usual social activities, and for the family to reduce their social contact with others, through shame or embarrassment with their behaviour. As they become increasingly dependent they may follow their relative around, often repeatedly asking the same questions. They may become incontinent or disturb others during the night. Their daily living skills also deteriorate. They may have difficulty in managing money and become progressively unable to wash, dress or even feed themselves. However, the pattern of problems varies widely between different individuals, and each person may behave in quite different ways at different periods of the illness.

21. Changes in daily routine and life events often lead to more rapid deterioration of functioning (Ref. 23). If people with dementia are forced to move to a new location they can become depressed or disturbed (Ref. 24). This has implications for service providers, who may find that such moves lead to problems for themselves and the people in their care.

Prevalence of dementia

22. The prevalence of dementia rises sharply with age, with the proportion roughly doubling with every five years up to the age of 90. Recent estimates for England and Wales have been based on national census data and on surveys in six geographical areas (Refs. 25 and 26). The surveys found 6 per cent of 75–79 year olds, 13 per cent of 80–84 year olds and 25 per cent of those over 85 to have 'case level' dementia [EXHIBIT 1]. Approximately 11 per cent of those with dementia needed 'long interval care', nearly 50 per cent 'short interval care' and 34 per cent 'critical interval care'.

23. Dementia is more common in women than in men, especially in the older age groups. The rate of cognitive problems has been found to be higher in people of lower social class and lower educational achievement. A model for predicting the prevalence of dementia in local areas, based on age profiles of local populations, has been developed on the basis of a national survey of disability, and has been validated by comparison with local surveys (Ref. 25).

24. In 1996, it was estimated that 34 per cent of people with dementia were in hospital, residential care or nursing homes. The number of people with dementia in such establishments is expected to increase by 14 per cent over the next ten years (if the criteria for admission remain the same). One-third of those with severe dementia (in need of constant care or supervision) live in community settings, supported mainly by their spouses or children. This amounts to around 200,000 people (Ref. 27). In one local authority, two-thirds of those living in residential care in the early 1980s were found to have dementia, one-half of them severe dementia (Ref. 28). This figure is likely to have risen during the 1990s. Another survey found 15 per cent of those receiving home care in one borough had dementia (Ref. 29).

EXHIBIT 1

Estimated prevalence of dementia

Dementia rises sharply with age.

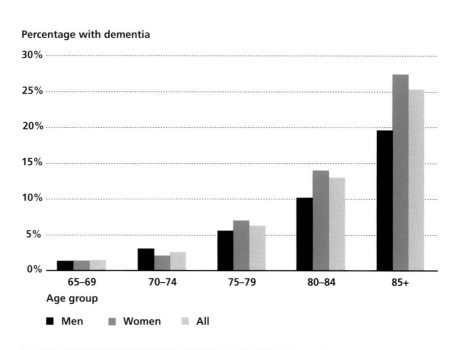

Percentage with dementia

Age group

■ Men ■ Women ▨ All

Source: MRC CFA study

Depression is the most common mental health problem in older people

Depression

25. Depression and other mental health problems are sometimes called functional mental illnesses, as they are not usually associated with major physical degeneration of the brain cells. Clinical depression differs from the kind of depressed mood experienced by everyone at times – by its intensity, duration and the degree to which it interferes with ordinary life.

Prevalence of depression

26. Depression is the most common mental health problem in older people, with women likely to be depressed more often than men. Between 10 and 16 per cent of people over 65 in three major cities were found to have symptoms of depression (Refs.30–33), compared with only 9 per cent of younger adults in the Office of Population Censuses and Surveys (OPCS) survey for Great Britain (Ref. 34). People who are depressed are more likely than others to commit suicide, especially men over 85 (Ref. 35).

27. Older people are more likely to become depressed if they are in poor health, lack social support and experience either prolonged difficulties over a period of time (for example, poverty, poor housing, disability) or have care responsibilities for a disabled relative (Refs. 36 and 37). So, the local prevalence of depression varies with the characteristics of the area, such as poverty and the percentage of older people living alone. Those caring for a disabled relative are at high risk, as around one-third experience clinical depression (Ref. 38). Major life events such as bereavement, experienced by many older people, can also lead to depression (Ref. 39).

28. Depression is also very common among people in residential and nursing care. Around 40 per cent were found to be clinically depressed, but only a small minority of these receive specific drug treatment or counselling to help them (Ref. 28). One-quarter of those receiving home care are depressed, but only a few of these are receiving treatment (Ref. 40), despite the fact that death rates are significantly higher among those who are depressed than those who are not, and that appropriate treatment with drugs and psychological therapies can help them significantly (Refs. 41 and 42). Identifying depression correctly is important, as it is often mistaken for dementia.

Others with mental health needs

29. A small number of people who developed a severe and enduring mental health problem when young, such as schizophrenia, are growing older. Some of these have spent many years living in institutions and may have been resettled into alternative supported accommodation. Others have spent most of their lives in the community, but have experienced many hospital admissions over the years. Many are physically frail and need considerable support, so they may be living in specialist residential or nursing homes (Ref. 43).

Minority ethnic groups

30. The age profile for minority ethnic groups in Britain is usually different from that of the indigenous population, and varies with the group, depending on their pattern of emigration to Britain. A community survey in Liverpool identified more ethnic minority people in the 65–74 age band but fewer over 75 (Ref. 44). The rate of depression in some groups, such as Bengali people, older black African and particularly Somali people, is higher than for white British people (Ref. 45). Dementia may also be higher in some ethnic groups, especially non-English speaking black Africans and Chinese – although the survey findings may not be reliable, due to difficulties in the interview approach (Ref. 44).

31. The commonly held assumption that minority ethnic and black families 'look after their own' and have less need for services is not necessarily borne out (Ref. 46). One-third of an African-Caribbean group surveyed had no children in this country, and the families of many others were too busy working to care for them. Even where extended family networks exist, caring at home is largely carried out by one person, who may be under great stress, as is the case in most indigenous British families. Where formal support is provided by service agencies, any extended family support tends to decrease (Ref. 47). However, formal services can sometimes be insensitive to cultural norms and may threaten carers' well-being if they do not reinforce the carer's role in an appropriate manner.

Users' and carers' needs

People with dementia

32. On average, people with dementia live for seven or eight years after the problem has been first diagnosed, although there are wide individual variations (Ref. 48). They and their families have to deal with the effects of the dementia itself, leading to a deterioration in memory, reasoning and, ability and also the changes in relationships and interactions as other people begin to treat them differently. They have the same basic human needs as anyone else – needs for comfort, attachment, inclusion, occupation and identity (Ref. 49) – so services need to consider these if they are to help.

33. Many of the carers of older people with dementia are themselves fairly old. Up to 60 per cent are husbands or wives (Ref. 38). Carers of people with dementia generally experience greater stress than carers of people with other kinds of need, nearly one-half having some kind of mental health problem themselves (Ref. 50). The ability of carers to tolerate difficult behaviour is the critical factor in their asking for help from statutory services (Ref. 51). Many feel that their needs for home support and medical care are not fully met (Ref. 50). The most difficult problems for carers to cope with are personality changes, lack of everyday conversation, criticism, excessive demands and difficult behaviour such as aggression, disturbance at night, incontinence and wandering (Refs. 52 and 53).

34. The way in which services are run locally can make all the difference to carers' ability and desire to continue caring. They generally value emotional support above all other kinds of help, but also need information about the nature of the illness, the services available and how to gain access to them (Ref. 54). Contact with a trusted professional who can arrange for services to be provided, facilitate choice and assist with claiming benefits, is usually the most helpful. When it comes to choosing residential care they need to know about the kinds of needs that are best catered for in specific homes, not just a simple list of the homes in the area (Ref. 55). The support and information provided by self-help groups such as the ADS is also highly valued. Carers from minority ethnic groups are more likely than others to have difficulty in accepting and using services such as day and respite care unless they are provided in a culturally sensitive manner. Support from a professional who understands their difficulties is, therefore, particularly important. A list of ten key requirements of carers has been identified by the National Institute for Social Work (Ref. 56):

1. Early identification of problems.
2. Comprehensive assessment of needs for help, including social and medical needs.
3. Medical treatment for any treatable problems.
4. Prompt referral to other services that can provide help.
5. Information, advice and counselling.
6. Continuing support and review, ideally from a known and trusted individual.
7. Regular help with domestic and personal care tasks.
8. Regular breaks from caring.
9. Financial support.
10. Permanent residential care when it becomes necessary.

People with functional mental health problems

35. People with functional mental health problems may have intermittent periods of difficulty over many years or may recover altogether after a few months. Many can benefit from appropriate drugs or psychological treatments such as cognitive behavioural therapy (CBT) or bereavement counselling. Their carers often experience emotional and interpersonal difficulties, as well as practical difficulties in dealing with household tasks and finances. The users, when asked, are normally able to express their own needs and wishes, many of which are similar to those of younger people with mental health problems. The priorities of this group include:

• information about services and treatments;

• respect, dignity and confidentiality;

• a choice of appropriate services at times when they are needed;

- education and training for participation in service planning; and
- involvement in decisions about their care and services in general (Ref. 57).

In addition, isolation is often a major problem for older people with depression, so spending time with others or having a regular visitor can make a great deal of difference to their well-being, even though it will not 'cure' the depression.

The services

36. There are three key aims of mental health services for older people.

1. To maintain the mental health of older people and to help to preserve their independence.

2. To support family carers as well as the older people themselves.

3. To provide intermittent or permanent residential care for those who are so disabled that this is the most practical and humane way of looking after them (Ref. 58).

37. A range of services can be provided in any local area to meet the needs of users and carers [EXHIBIT 2, overleaf], although not all are available everywhere. A number of different agencies are involved, so services are accountable to different managers and the funding comes from a number of sources. Some specialise in caring for older people with mental health problems, but others provide for this group as well as older people with a range of different needs. Specialist services have the advantage of staff who have been trained to deal with the needs of people with mental health problems, although some general services are also able to provide high quality care. People at an early stage of their illness may prefer to use general services that do not carry a mental health label. Good communication between the agencies, and pooling of their resources where possible, is crucial to the development of local services that fully meet local needs. Otherwise, older people and their carers may not receive the help they need, when they need it.

38. The health authority normally commissions an NHS trust to provide a specialist service for older people with mental health problems, including:

- psychiatrists of old age;
- community mental health teams (CMHTs) of professionals such as community psychiatric nurses (CPNs), psychologists, occupational therapists (OTs) and physiotherapists;
- community professionals not in CMHTs;
- outpatient clinics;
- day hospitals; and
- hospital beds for acute care, respite care and possibly continuing care.

Primary Care Groups (PCGs) and primary care teams will become increasingly involved in commissioning health services, including 'packages' of care for individuals with complex needs.

EXHIBIT 2

The range of possible services

Not all services are available everywhere.

Source: Audit Commission

GPs have often known people for many years

39. GPs and other primary care staff play a very important role, especially in the early stages. They have often known people for many years and are usually the first professionals with whom they and their relatives discuss emerging problems. GPs can make referrals to specialists, carry out initial assessments and investigate any possible physical causes of their problems. They may also give support and advice, as well as prescribe medication, before the situation reaches a stage where more help is needed. Once someone is receiving care from specialist services, the GP continues to have a role in monitoring progress and in providing physical health care.

40. The local authority social services department normally commissions and/or provides:

- social workers or care managers;
- home-care workers;
- mobile meals;
- day care;
- residential respite care for periods of a few days to a few weeks;
- residential care; and
- nursing home care.

Social services provision tends to focus mainly on those with dementia and others with long-term conditions. In some areas joint resource centres are being developed by health and social service agencies.

41. Acute and geriatric health services provide care for large numbers of people with mental health problems who also have physical problems. Sometimes mental health problems only become apparent when people have been admitted to hospital for their physical needs. So, these services are a major source of referrals, and liaison between them and mental health specialists is vital. In a few areas there are specialist wards for those with both mental and physical health problems. Younger people with dementia are usually dependent on the specialist services for older people with mental health problems, even though some of their needs may be quite different. Access to special provision is particularly important for this group.

42. Local voluntary organisations, such as the ADS or Age Concern, or community groups, may provide additional services, some of which may be funded by social services or the health authority. These can include:

- care in people's homes that enables carers to take a break;
- day care;
- carers' support groups; and
- advocacy and advice for carers and users.

43. Social security payments are an important source of support for older people with mental health problems and their families. The main benefits they are likely to receive are Attendance Allowance (a lower rate for people needing help during the day and a higher rate for those needing 24 hour care), Invalid Care Allowance (for carers under 65 whose relatives receive attendance allowance), housing benefit and income support.

Costs of care

44. Estimates of the costs of care for people with dementia vary, the differences being due mainly to the inclusion, in some, of 'informal care' by unpaid carers, usually close family members, but not in others. The former establish the cost of the opportunities lost by carers looking after people living at home. Without this 'informal care' the cost to public services would be considerably higher than it is at present. One study estimated a total of £6.1 billion (at 1998/99 prices) for the 320,000 people in England[1] with 'advanced cognitive impairment', based on the 1991 OPCS survey. Of this, £3.3 billion falls to health and social services [EXHIBIT 3] (Ref. 59). Most of these people live in the community, 13 per cent living alone, 50 per cent with others, and 37 per cent in residential settings (NHS, local authority, nursing homes and other residential homes). The cost of caring for someone in a long-stay hospital ward was £890 per week, compared with £390 in a residential home or £290 at home with others. Another study estimated the cost of caring for people with Alzheimer's Disease in England to be just over £1 billion (Ref. 60) of which 66 per cent was accounted for by residential care, and 25 per cent by hospital services.

45. The costs of health and social services care for individual older people 'living in the community' are higher for those with dementia than those with other mental health problems, according to a study in one London borough. But since depression is more common – 15 per cent, compared with 6 per cent for dementia – the total costs for this group are higher [EXHIBIT 4] (Ref. 61). Few of those with depression were receiving appropriate treatment – either with drugs or other therapies. Better treatment could result in significant cost savings, as people who recover from depression tend to use fewer services (Ref. 62).

46. Getting the most appropriate services to meet the needs of users and carers depends on how easily they gain access to help. Ways to identify the problem and to get help are explored in the next chapter.

---

1   No comparable information is available for Wales.

EXHIBIT 3

Total costs of care for people with dementia (England, 98/99 prices)

Health and social services spent a total of £3.3 billion on care.

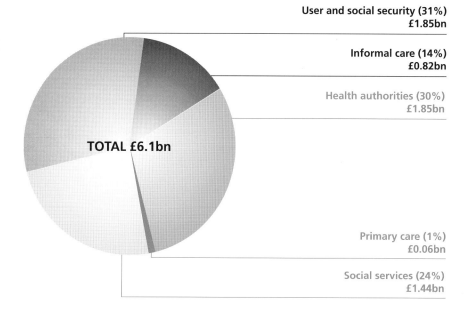

User and social security (31%)
£1.85bn

Informal care (14%)
£0.82bn

Health authorities (30%)
£1.85bn

TOTAL £6.1bn

Primary care (1%)
£0.06bn

Social services (24%)
£1.44bn

Source: Kavanagh et al, 1993 (Ref. 59)

EXHIBIT 4

The costs of health and social services care for people in the community with mental health problems in one local authority

The total costs are highest for those with depression.

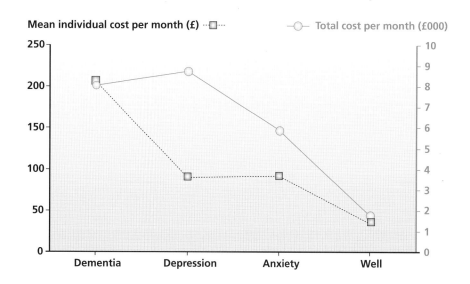

Mean individual cost per month (£)   Total cost per month (£000)

Source: Livingston et al, 1997 (Ref. 61)

2

Identification and Initial Responses by Services

Carers usually want to know what the problem is as early as possible, and how to get help when they need it. GPs and primary care teams are a crucial point of contact, but they often need more support and advice from specialist mental health professionals. Providing local information and support for carers is also essential.

Identifying and understanding the problem

47. Those caring for older people with mental health problems are usually the first to call for help – usually as the result of growing stress. The way services respond can make all the difference to carers' ability to continue caring, but the problem most commonly voiced by carers is difficulty in getting access to information and help in the first place. One carer described a four-year wait, while she cared for her highly dependent mother, before any support services were offered. Carers usually want to know the diagnosis and how it is likely to progress, as early as possible.

> *'We do not know yet what waits around the corner.'*
>
> *'I would like someone I can talk to about my husband's illness, and advice about the future as he gets worse and even harder to cope with.'*
> (Audit Commission survey)

Early identification of mental health problems

48. GPs and other primary care staff play a very important role, as they are usually the first port of call for information and help. They can give support and advice, as well as prescribe medication, before specialist care is needed. They are becoming even more important as PCGs in England and local health groups in Wales become more involved in commissioning specialist services. Over 1,000 GPs responded to a survey by the Audit Commission,[1] a 55 per cent response rate [TABLE 1, overleaf]. However, only around one-half believed that it was important to look actively for early signs of dementia and to make an early diagnosis. Many of the others said they saw no point in looking for an incurable condition – even though carers could be helped by early advice. Their comments included:

> *'What is the point in looking for an untreatable illness?'*
>
> *'Dementia is untreatable, so why diagnose it?'*
>
> *'Diagnosing dementia can be difficult, uncertain and create unnecessary anxiety.'*
> (Audit Commission survey)

In contrast, almost nine out of ten believed it was important to look for early signs of depression and to make a diagnosis, although research shows that it is often missed in general practice.

49. GPs should be alert to early signs of memory problems, confusion or depression in their routine practice when older people, especially those over 75, consult them for any health problem. They need to be able to recognise dementia and to distinguish it from confusion due to physical ill-health. They should have protocols to follow, perhaps provided by local specialist services. They should also consider screening carers for signs of depression. The roles of practice nurses and health visitors may usefully be expanded to promote this area of work. The GPs who believed that local mental health services for older people were good

---

1   Adapted from a survey methodology developed by the University of Kent at Canterbury (Ref. 13).

*Less than one-half of
the GPs surveyed felt
that they had received
sufficient training to
help them diagnose
and manage dementia*

were also more likely to believe in the value of early diagnosis.[1] Local service providers should consult GPs to find out their views on local services and whether such services reflect the requirements and practices of GPs' patients.

Training

50. GPs need to be suitably trained if they are to recognise mental health problems in older people, but many felt ill-prepared to deal with them. Less than one-half of those surveyed felt that they had received sufficient training to help them diagnose and manage dementia. In contrast, GPs felt more confident about dealing with depression, and two-thirds felt their training was adequate to manage it, even though they often fail to identify the condition. Those providing specialist mental health services for older people should make special efforts to contact GPs – especially those who make few referrals – and offer support and training. Locally provided postgraduate training for GPs and other members of the primary care team should help them to identify and deal with mental health problems in older people. Primary care professionals also need help in identifying how and when to disclose information to carers and users in a way that is supportive and minimises distress. Such training was provided by specialist services in only three out of the 12 study sites [EXHIBIT 5].

I   Pearson correlation, significant at .01 level.

TABLE 1

The survey of GPs in 12 areas

Statement	Percentage of GPs who agree with the statement in relation to:	
	Dementia	Depression
It is important to look actively for early signs of…	54	88
It is beneficial to make an early diagnosis of…	52	92
I use specific tests and/or protocols to help me diagnose and manage…	44	35
I have ready access, when required, to specialist advice to help me diagnose and manage…	75	69
There are satisfactory specialised services for older people, and/or their families, in my area to meet the needs of people with…	50	51
I have received sufficient basic and post-qualifying training to help me diagnose and manage…	48	70

EXHIBIT 5

Contact with and training for GPs

Training was provided by specialist services in only 3 out of the 12 study sites.

	A	B	C	D	E	F	G	H	J	K	L	M
	STUDY SITES											
Training for GPs (eg, use of screening tools, treatment of depression, mental health promotion)	X	X	X	X	X	X	X	✓	X	✓	✓	X
Links between CMHTs and GP practices, via named workers	X	X	✓	X	X	X	X	X	X	X	✓	X
Links between social services and GP practices, via named workers	✓	X	✓	✓	✓	X	X	X	X	X	X	X
Positive efforts to educate and contact GPs	X	X	✓	X	X	✓	✓	X	✓	✓	X	X

Source: Audit Commission study sites

51. Fewer than one-half of the GPs questioned said that they used specific tests or protocols to help them to diagnose dementia – for example, the Mini Mental State Examination, (MMSE). Only one-third said that they used specific tests or protocols for depression – for example, the Geriatric Depression Scale (GDS) (Ref. 63). These tests provide standard questions and ways to score them. Scores within a certain range indicate the likely presence of mental health problems. GPs in some areas were more likely to use such tests than in others [EXHIBIT 6, overleaf]. In areas where few GPs use them, mental health professionals should make particular efforts to work with local primary care staff and to provide guidance in the use of protocols for the identification of dementia and depression.

EXHIBIT 6

Percentage of GPs in different areas who use specific tests or protocols to diagnose dementia or depression

GPs in some areas were more likely to use such tests than in others.

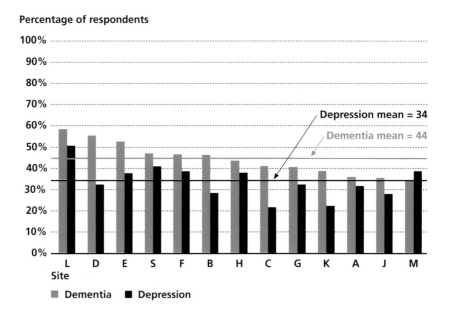

Source: Audit Commission GP survey

52. In addition to tests such as the MMSE and GDS, protocols that give guidelines for further investigation and action can be helpful. In one site visited, the health authority had been developing a 'dementia care pathway' and monitoring its use. Providing a protocol is only part of the answer, as individual professionals need encouragement or incentives to use it. They may also need training in how to apply tests sensitively and appropriately to the situation of the individual and their family. Some minority ethnic groups, for example, may find such tests particularly difficult. Looking for risk factors, such as bereavement, isolation and physical health problems, is also important. A project initiated by the University of Bristol developed a detailed protocol for the identification and management of dementia in primary care, but its use varied widely [**EXHIBIT 7**]. Where individual GPs had been actively involved in its development they were using it regularly (1 GP identified over 15 new cases in a year), but colleagues, even within the same practice, who had not been involved, were not (5 new cases identified between 4 GPs in the same period). Further research is needed on the effects of earlier identification and diagnosis on the outcomes and on the satisfaction of users and carers.

EXHIBIT 7

Protocol for the identification and management of dementia in primary care

Where individual GPs had been involved in its development, they were using it regularly.

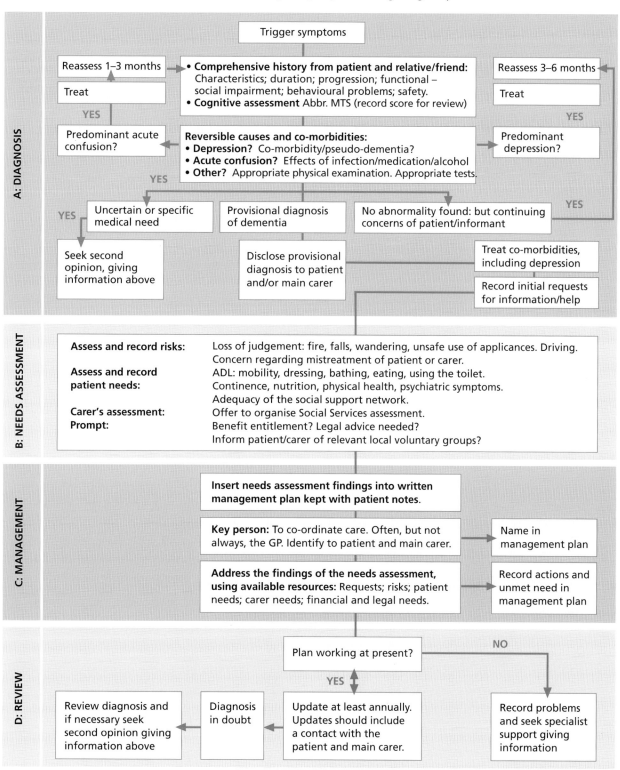

Source: *University of Bristol, Division of Primary Care*

Consultants and others from mental health services should encourage GPs and primary care teams to use standard assessment tests... by offering training and support

53. GPs who believed in the value of looking for early signs of dementia and in making an early diagnosis were significantly more likely to use tests or protocols.[I] This was also true for depression.[II] GPs who felt that they had received sufficient training to deal with these conditions were also significantly more likely to use specific tests or protocols.[III] If local mental health professionals were to provide local training, GPs might use standard tests more often and so improve the frequency and accuracy with which they identify mental health problems.

54. One approach to providing training has been a national programme for GPs and other primary care staff in 24 areas of the UK (Ref. 64). Around 300 GPs and 150 district nurses attended a series of one-day workshops. They were held on Saturdays, which may have helped to boost the attendance. The GPs were most interested in learning how to reach a diagnosis of dementia and also in how to initiate and co-ordinate support services, which was a problem for many.

55. Consultants and others from mental health services should encourage GPs and primary care teams to use standard assessment tests, such as the MMSE and GDS, by offering training and support. The training should cover how to apply the tests appropriately and sensitively as well as how to look for signs of depression in the carers, and initiate support services. They should also provide guidance on how best to inform carers and users. Commissioners of services should encourage the use of protocols to aid the identification of mental health problems in primary care. Undergraduate medical training should also incorporate these issues.

Support for GPs

56. Support for GPs from local mental health professionals is key, but it is patchy across the country. Around three-quarters of GPs believe they have access to advice, but in one site only one-third felt that advice was available [EXHIBIT 8]. GPs who felt they had access to specialist advice on both dementia and depression were significantly more likely to believe in the value of early diagnosis.[IV] There was also a significant relationship between the availability of specialist advice for depression and a belief in the value of early diagnosis.[V] Professionals working in specialist services need to communicate with local GPs to provide advice and support.

57. Having specialist workers linked to GP practices can help communication. The CMHTs for older people in only 2 of the 12 study sites were using individual link workers to liaise with particular

I   Pearson correlations of 0.12 and 0.13.

II   Pearson correlations of 0.17 and 0.15.

III   Pearson correlations of 0.26 and 0.11 respectively.

IV   Both Pearson correlations of .089.

V   Correlations of 0.17 and 0.15.

EXHIBIT 8

GPs' agreement with the statement 'I have ready access, when required, to specialist advice to help me diagnose and manage dementia/depression' in different areas

In one site, only one-third felt that advice was available.

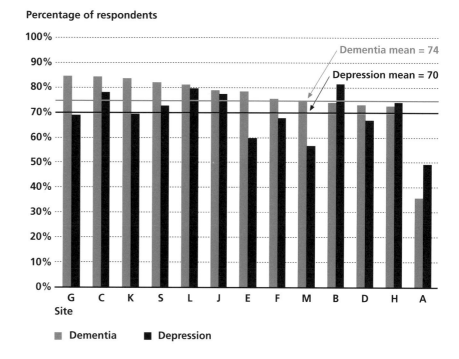

Percentage of respondents

Dementia mean = 74

Depression mean = 70

Site

■ Dementia   ■ Depression

Source: Audit Commission GP survey

GP practices [**EXHIBIT 5, p23**]. Social services provided link workers for particular GP practices in four study sites. In these four sites, the GPs were more likely to say that they had ready access to specialist advice to help them to diagnose and to manage dementia and depression, and that there were satisfactory specialised services, than in other sites.[I]

58. Special initiatives to contact GPs at intervals can be useful. In five sites, staff of the mental health services for older people had made particular efforts to contact and provide education and support for GPs in their area. GPs in these sites more often said that they had ready access to specialist advice to help them to diagnose and manage dementia and depression and also that there were satisfactory specialised services than in other sites.[II] This demonstrates the value of specialist staff making contact with GP practices and responding to their needs for information and support. In North Tyneside, GPs are contacted regularly and their referrals monitored [**CASE STUDY 1, overleaf**].

59. Those providing specialist mental health services for older people should make special and repeated efforts to contact GPs who refer very few people, and offer them support and training. Commissioners of specialist services should ensure that this happens.

I   All significant at .005 level, using Student's t-Test.

II   First statement significant at .005 level, second statement at .005 level for dementia and .05 level for depression, using Student's t-Test.

> **CASE STUDY 1**
>
> **Supporting GPs in North Tyneside**
>
> - CMHT staff had provided a series of lectures for GPs.
> - They monitored the referral patterns from GPs across the patch to identify practices that referred very few people.
> - Local surveys of GPs' views and needs were carried out.
> - Practices that referred significantly fewer people or expressed a wish for support were targeted for a series of 'information roadshows' that went out to GP surgeries.

Informing and supporting carers

Providing information

60. Carers are the main supporters of older people with mental health problems, especially in the early stages. Many continue to care for highly dependent relatives as the condition progresses. They need clear information, including written information, to help them to understand what a diagnosis of dementia means and what is likely to happen in the future, as well as information about local services (Ref. 56). Users also need to know about the diagnosis and understand what it means to them. They may be able to plan better for the future if they are given sufficient information at an early stage. Sometimes a lack of knowledge adds to carers' stress. They may think, wrongly, that their relative is being deliberately difficult and awkward:

> *'I was sometimes impatient with my mother whereas better information would have helped me understand* (Ref. 65).*'*

> *'I would like greater knowledge of the help on offer.'*

> *'I need help to learn and to cope.'*
> (Audit Commission survey)

61. Providing clear information and training for carers can increase their knowledge, reduce stress and reduce their perceived unmet needs for resources, without necessarily increasing their use of resources (Ref. 66). Reducing the carer's stress may delay the user's admission to residential care (Ref. 67).

Reducing the carer's stress may delay the user's admission to residential care

62. Although GPs are highly respected, and their role in caring for older people is highly valued by users and carers, they often fail to provide adequate and helpful information. In one site, where GPs had been given information leaflets, some refused to make them available in their surgeries, for fear that they might become liable for any shortcomings in the services described. Several GPs said that they preferred to wait until they felt the carer was no longer coping adequately before making a referral for help or being explicit about the nature of the problem. In one local survey of carers, fewer than one in five found that the information given them by their GP was helpful (Ref. 65). Many carers said that they had not been informed about essential legal issues, such as Enduring Power of Attorney, by GPs or other service providers, but had learned about this through a chance meeting with another carer.

'I would like to be given answers when I ask questions.'
(Audit Commission survey)

Since this is no one professional's responsibility it tends to be left out. Better co-ordination between professionals from different agencies should help to fill such gaps.

63. Sometimes the GP thought he/she had told the relatives the diagnosis of dementia, but relatives reported only being told about 'poor memory' or 'confusion' and did not realise the full implications (Ref. 68). Carers need to be told about a diagnosis of dementia in a sensitive and appropriate manner, then contacted again some time later to make sure that they understand the implications.

'I need more information.'
(Audit Commission survey)

64. When carers are asked for their views, the lack of suitable information and support for them becomes obvious. Only 50 per cent of 850 carers of people with dementia who completed an Audit Commission survey said that they were told about the diagnosis soon after their relative started to become confused and only 44 per cent said that they were told how it was likely to affect them in the future [EXHIBIT 9, overleaf]. Less than one-half were asked if they needed any help. This varied from less than 30 per cent in some sites to around 60 per cent in others. Around one-third were told about the legal rights and responsibilities that could apply (such as Enduring Power of Attorney) and one-third had been told how to care for their relative and cope with dementia. Of those surveyed, 56 per cent had been introduced at an early stage to someone they could contact whenever they had a problem. These rather worrying findings reflected the views of carers whose relatives were receiving care from mental health services. Those not yet in contact with specialist services would be likely to indicate they had received even less information and help from primary or specialist care. Those who had been contacted through the ADS were less likely than other carers to say that they had received the information they needed.

EXHIBIT 9

Carers' views about the information given to them

Less than one-half were asked if they needed any help.

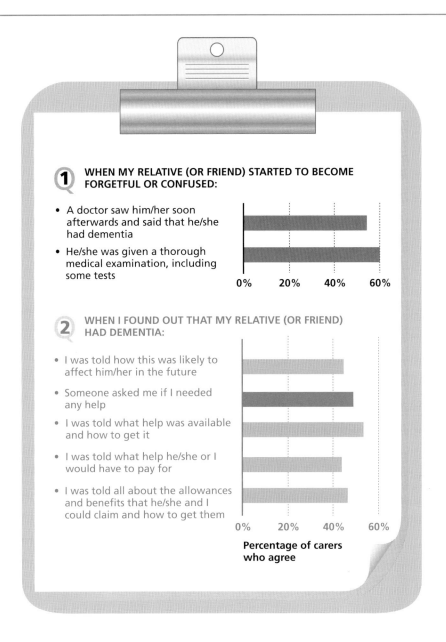

1 Q WHEN MY RELATIVE (OR FRIEND) STARTED TO BECOME FORGETFUL OR CONFUSED:

- A doctor saw him/her soon afterwards and said that he/she had dementia
- He/she was given a thorough medical examination, including some tests

0% 20% 40% 60%

2 WHEN I FOUND OUT THAT MY RELATIVE (OR FRIEND) HAD DEMENTIA:

- I was told how this was likely to affect him/her in the future
- Someone asked me if I needed any help
- I was told what help was available and how to get it
- I was told what help he/she or I would have to pay for
- I was told all about the allowances and benefits that he/she and I could claim and how to get them

0% 20% 40% 60%

Percentage of carers who agree

Source: Audit Commission carers' survey

65. Information about mental health was available for carers in GP surgeries in only 4 of the 12 study sites and information about local services in 5 sites. In six, information was provided elsewhere, such as at a public library or carers' centre [EXHIBIT 10]. In site D, an information service was provided for carers, funded by the health authority, but it was still difficult for people to get access to information when they needed it. In site C, a telephone helpline was commissioned from a neighbouring authority, but little was known about how much use was being made of it. In site H, leaflets were distributed that gave the telephone number of a voluntary organisation that could link up with other services.

EXHIBIT 10

Information available to carers and users

Information about mental health was provided in GP surgeries in only four study sites.

		A	B	C	D	E	F	G	H	J	K	L	M
	STUDY SITES												
Information available for carers/users in GP surgeries	about mental health services	X	X	✓	X	X	X	✓	X	✓	✓	X	N/K
	about local services	X	X	✓	X	X	X	✓	X	✓	✓	✓	X
Information available for carers/users from somewhere other than GP surgeries		X	X	✓	✓	X	X	✓	X	✓	X	✓	✓
Information available for carers/users in different languages		N/K	X	X	X	X	X	X	X	✓	X	✓	X
Advocacy available for carers/users		X	X	X	X	X	X	X	X	✓	✓	✓	✓

Note: N/K= Not known

Source: Audit Commission checklist for study sites

66. However, some examples of good practice were found. In Wirral, a course was run for carers [CASE STUDY 2, overleaf]. Although this was only able to reach those who were already in touch with specialist services, it was highly valued by those who participated. Providing alternative care for people with a mental health problem is essential if carers are to be able to attend support groups and courses.

67. Those providing and commissioning specialist mental health services for older people should ensure that there is a co-ordinated approach to the provision of competent advice and information to carers and users. Information, in languages and formats that can be understood easily by local people, should be distributed to GP surgeries and other public places. Local groups or voluntary organisations should be consulted about what is written in information leaflets and may choose to provide it themselves. The ADS can provide informative and helpful leaflets. A telephone service can be a useful supplement to written information. Service providers should also consider providing lectures and training/education courses for carers.

CASE STUDY 2

The Wirral carers' course

Members of the CMHT ran an eight week course, 'coping with caring', with guest speakers from statutory services, voluntary organisations and others such as pharmacists. Each year 4 courses were run and there was usually a waiting list of around 20 people wanting to attend. The social services day centre was able to care for some service users while their relatives attended the course.

Support for carers

68. The importance of emotional and practical support for carers, from people who understand their situation, has already been noted (Ref. 54).

'I need someone to talk to who deals with people with dementia.'

'...More social contact...'

'...Support and information...'
(Audit Commission survey)

69. Counselling and support for carers were available in 5 of the 12 sites, run in 3 of them by the local ADS group. Advocacy, to represent the views of users and carers to professionals and to provide advice in matters such as benefits, was available in four study sites. Where support for carers was available, it was usually focused on those caring for someone with dementia. Support for carers of those with other problems was less common.

70. Carers' organisations and support groups, such as ADS, can provide very useful support and information to users and carers, independently of statutory services. Carers' support groups, for example, are often the main sources of information about benefit entitlements, such as Attendance Allowance and Invalid Care Allowance, and legal matters such as Enduring Power of Attorney. Some are local branches of national organisations such as ADS or Age Concern. Advocates from these organisations may be able to help carers find their way around the benefits system and perhaps to provide volunteer support on a long-term basis. However, carers' organisations and advocacy services should not become a substitute for statutory services, as seemed to be happening in one area. Here, the carers' and advocates' representatives described themselves as a 'safety net', providing care when social services had been unable to help, as had occurred in one recent case. This was different from voluntary organisations being commissioned to provide a specific service such as day care, where the strategic responsibility remains with the statutory sector.

71. In North Tyneside, a carers' centre had been developed [CASE STUDY 3]. In Bromley an information and support service for carers provides information and a range of support services [CASE STUDY 4]. GPs should be encouraged to refer users and carers to support groups such as ADS, as early as possible.

The North Tyneside Carers' Centre

The centre was set up by social services and carers' organisations working together. Some funding was provided by the Princess Royal Trust. The centre houses a number of organisations, including a local branch of the ADS, a jointly run 'home sitting' service (with social services), an information and advice service and an advocacy project. The centre and its services are highly valued by carers. Although the advocacy project receives many referrals from statutory services, it provides an independent voice in matters such as appeals against admissions to hospital under the Mental Health Act 1983. However, it does not generally reach those who are not already receiving statutory services.

Bromley Carers Information and Support Service (CISS)

CISS provides a telephone information service to local carers and professionals, written leaflets and newsletters and a range of support services. In 1997/98 the enquiry line received over 2,000 telephone enquiries, 60 per cent of which were from carers. Information was provided about financial matters, especially benefits, local services and other issues such as transport.

CISS also provides locally based support workers, help with writing letters and filling in forms, a home respite scheme using trained community service volunteers, and a register of paid sitters who have been approved and are given support and training. A daily telephone check-in line is available to carers who look after someone who would be unable to call for help if the carer fell ill. Carers on the list call an answerphone with a code number every day. If they fail to do so, a neighbour will be called to check up on them and get help if necessary. A 'Carer's Card' can be carried, giving details of the person being cared for and the names of people who should be contacted in case of an emergency. A number of support groups exist, including one for carers of people with long-term mental health problems. CISS runs occasional training sessions for carers on a variety of topics such as specific mental illnesses, welfare benefits and other practical matters. A 'carers' working group' represents the views of carers in the area and campaigns for improvements to services.

CISS is a voluntary organisation, staffed by paid workers and volunteers. It has seven central staff and nine area-based workers. It is partly funded by the local authority and health authority, and receives grants from charitable trusts and local companies.

Other routes into services

72. Referrals to the mental health service can come from many different sources [EXHIBIT 11]. Accepting community referrals from sources other than the GP or another doctor can sometimes make a service more responsive to need. However, this was not happening in most of the sites visited. Users and carers could refer themselves to the service in only 2 of the 12 study sites. In Newry and Mourne in Northern Ireland [CASE STUDY 5], a number of approaches were used to try to meet the needs of GPs and users.

EXHIBIT 11

Sources of referral to mental health services
Referrals can come from many different sources.

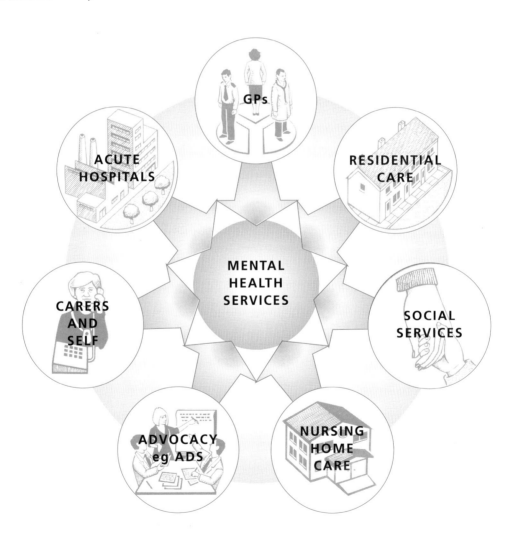

Source: Audit Commission

CASE STUDY 5

Newry and Mourne

The community trust employs both health and social services staff. All GP practices have a nominated link worker, usually a social work assistant, who takes all the referrals of older people to social services. The link worker can take referrals to the CMHT and for day care. Users and carers can also refer themselves to the team (but not to the consultant). The link worker can also facilitate referral to social services for other client groups.

A series of training seminars on dementia and local services have been held for GPs and other primary care staff, in conjunction with the local ADS group. A six-week training course was also run for carers, with more planned at six-monthly intervals. These were followed by a poster campaign and information evenings for the general public. The number of referrals from GPs has increased substantially since the start of the campaign.

The consultant has written to all GPs in the area, sending them copies of the MMSE, to be completed before a referral is sent to her. Since doing this, the use of the test has increased substantially. Each practice has been provided with leaflets for carers about dementia and the structure of local services.

Providing good services to refer people to

73. One reason that GPs may be reluctant to refer people with dementia is that they do not believe the local services are very helpful in meeting needs. On average, only one-half of the GPs surveyed thought that there were satisfactory specialist services available locally either for people with dementia or older people with depression, but this varied between areas [EXHIBIT 12]. Where the scores are particularly low, this implies that either the services or their relationships with local GPs are poor. GPs may have been dissatisfied with the availability and responsiveness of local services or the lack of co-ordination between them. They may have received some critical feedback from carers about the quality of services provided. Providers of specialist mental health services should survey the views of their local GPs from time to time, and aim to address any problems that are revealed. As people's conditions become more serious, they need more help, usually from a range of services providing support in their own homes, day care and outpatient provision, and residential and hospital beds. But the extent and quality of these vary. These variations and ways to improve the quality are explored in the next chapter.

EXHIBIT 12

GPs' agreement with the statement 'there are satisfactory specialised services for older people in my area'

On average, only one-half of the GPs thought that there were satisfactory specialised services available locally.

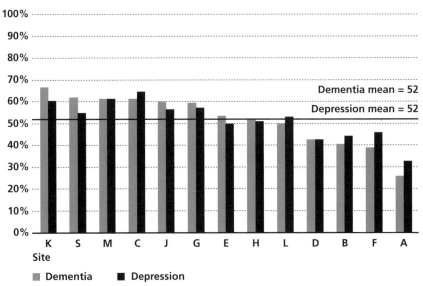

Percentage of respondents

Dementia mean = 52
Depression mean = 52

Site

■ Dementia ■ Depression

Source: Audit Commission GP survey

RECOMMENDATIONS

2   Identification and Initial Responses by Services

Helping GPs to identify problems

1 GPs should be alert to early signs of memory problems, confusion or depression in their routine practice when older people, especially those over 75, consult them for any health problem. They should have protocols to follow, perhaps provided by local specialist services. They should also consider screening carers for signs of depression. The role of health visitors may usefully be expanded to promote this area of work.

2 Local service providers should consult GPs to find out their views on local services and whether they reflect the requirements and practices of GPs.

3 Consultants and others from mental health services should encourage GPs and primary care teams to use standard assessment tests, such as the MMSE and GDS, by offering training and support. The training should cover how to apply the tests appropriately and sensitively as well as how to look for signs of depression in the carers. They should also provide guidance on how best to inform carers and users and to initiate support services. Commissioners of services should encourage the use of protocols to aid the identification of mental health problems in primary care. Undergraduate medical training should also incorporate these issues.

4 Those providing specialist mental health services for older people should make special and repeated efforts to contact GPs who refer very few people, and offer them support and training.

Providing information and help for carers

5 Those providing and commissioning specialist mental health services for older people should ensure that there is a co-ordinated approach for the provision of competent information and advice to carers and users. Information, in languages and formats that can be understood easily by local people, should be distributed to GP surgeries and other public places. Local groups or voluntary organisations should be consulted about what is written in information leaflets and may choose to provide it themselves. A telephone service can be a useful supplement to written information. Service providers should also consider providing lectures and training/education courses for carers.

6 GPs should be encouraged to refer users and carers to support groups such as ADS, as early as possible.

Improving specialist care

7 Providers of specialist mental health services should survey their local GPs from time to time, to find out their views on what can be done to address any problems that are revealed.

3———

Services to Help People at Home

The availability of specialist services and the way that they are used vary widely. Older people with mental health problems need a thorough assessment of needs – which is often best carried out at home – and access to a range of services to meet them. These might include specialist home care, outpatient clinics, memory clinics, specialist therapy, home-based or residential respite care, day treatment or long-term day care.

Expenditure

74. As people's conditions become more serious, they need more help, usually from specialist services. They need a range of services providing support in their own homes, day care and out-patient provision, and residential and hospital beds. The overall expenditure on specialist mental health services for older people varies from over £2.5 million to only £300,000 per 10,000 elderly population in different sites [EXHIBIT 13, overleaf]. Areas with few specialist services rely on general provision for older people, but support for primary care and care for people at home is usually best provided through specialisation. Most of the expenditure on specialist services comes from health, rather than social services, and goes on hospital and residential care. But most people prefer to be supported in their own homes, if they are given the choice. So, authorities and trusts need to respond to this by considering a shift in the balance towards community-based care. Using resources differently, to provide more home-based services, could help to meet their needs more effectively.

Home-based services

Specialist community staff

75. As most people prefer to remain at home for as long as possible, they rely on good community-based services. The CMHT is usually at the core of the specialist services, involving a mix of professionals (psychiatrists, community psychiatric nurses, social workers etc.) often from a range of agencies. It is this team that should provide support to GPs and links to other services. The number and mix of specialist community-based staff available varied considerably between study sites. In one site, for example, there were fewer CPNs and medical staff but more specialist social services staff [EXHIBIT 14, overleaf]. In this site, the agencies worked closely together and were in the process of developing a joint health and social care trust. This may have made it easier for staff to share expertise and to take on tasks in a more flexible way than traditional arrangements allow. The mental health service for older people in 8 of the 12 areas had multidisciplinary teams, while the remaining areas had only CPN teams. Authorities and trusts should review together the mix of staff they deploy and re-balance where necessary.

EXHIBIT 13

Expenditure on specialist mental health services for older people by all agencies in different sites (a) by health and social services (b) by home-based, outpatient/day and hospital/residential

Most of the expenditure on specialist services comes from health, rather than social services...

A

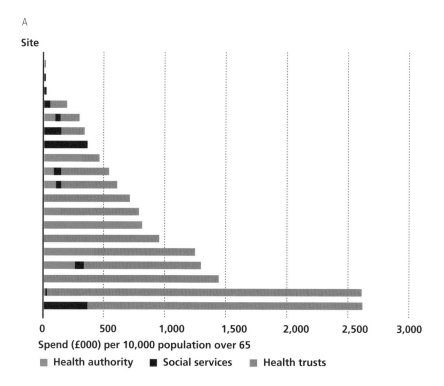

Site

Spend (£000) per 10,000 population over 65

■ Health authority ■ Social services ■ Health trusts

...and most goes on hospital and residential care.

B

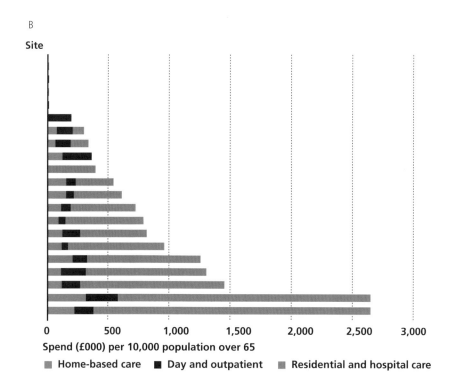

Site

Spend (£000) per 10,000 population over 65

■ Home-based care ■ Day and outpatient ■ Residential and hospital care

Source: Audit Commission resource mapping survey

EXHIBIT 14

The number of professional staff
(a) psychiatrists (b) CPNs and other
health professionals (c) social
workers

The number of specialist community-
based staff available varied
considerably.

A

FTE psychiatric medical staff

■ Consultants   ■ Senior/Specialist medical staff   ■ Other medical staff

B

FTE health professionals

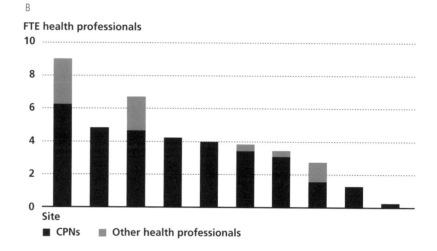

■ CPNs   ■ Other health professionals

C

FTE social work staff

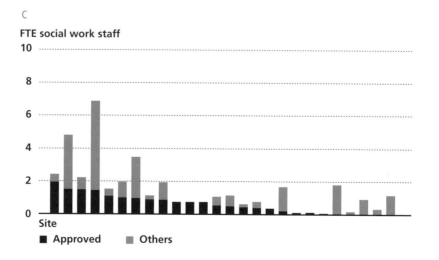

■ Approved   ■ Others

*Source: Audit Commission resource
mapping survey*

41

For people to be successfully supported at home, comprehensive assessment is an essential first step

People supported by community services

76. Information for this study was gathered on a sample of over 500 people living in the community and receiving care from community mental health professionals. In all 12 sites, the professionals were asked to complete a proforma, giving details of at least 22 people on their caseload, selected alphabetically to provide a random sample. Of those caseloads examined, 98 per cent of users were white European, 1 per cent black British or African-Caribbean and 1 per cent South Asian. Thirty-eight per cent of those with dementia and 41 per cent of those with a functional mental illness were living with an informal carer, usually a close family member. People with functional illnesses are more likely to be able to undertake personal and domestic tasks for themselves, as is indicated by a lower average dependency score on the Clifton Assessment Procedures for the Elderly Behaviour Rating Scale (CAPE) (Ref. 69). The mean score for those with dementia was 15, indicating high dependency, while the mean score for those with functional illness was much lower at 7.

77. The mean CAPE dependency score for people on community caseloads varied widely [**EXHIBIT 15**]. A high mean score indicates that services in some areas may be supporting very dependent people in their own homes in the community. There was no single factor that made it possible to support more dependent people in the community, but the availability of good quality care, such as specialist home care, day provision with extended hours, respite care and sitting services in the person's home, all contributed. In these areas, people with lower dependency may have been supported by generic social services care. Service managers should monitor caseloads on a regular basis and the dependency of people supported. This

EXHIBIT 15

CAPE scores for people in the community

The mean CAPE dependency score varied widely.

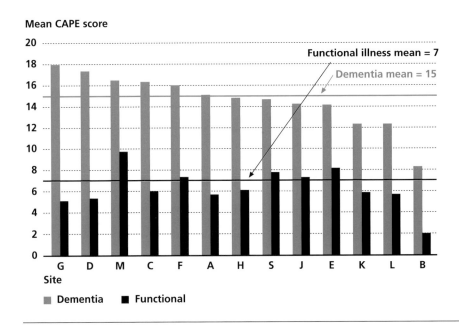

Source: Audit Commission individual case information survey

is one of the ways in which commissioners and providers can determine whether their service objectives, such as supporting highly dependent individuals at home, are being achieved.

Home assessments

78. For people to be successfully supported at home, comprehensive assessment is an essential first step. Assessment at home is often better as people are more likely to behave and communicate in their normal way in familiar surroundings. Staff can also build a more accurate picture of people's needs and learn the views of their carers. Professionals can observe whether there is adequate food in the house, whether people can make themselves a hot drink, and whether there are any likely risks from poor hygiene or fire hazards. A first full assessment should lead to an overview of the whole situation and a diagnosis, if this has not been provided by previous contacts. It should also become the first stage of care management. The first assessment should lead to an approximate prognosis or expectation of developments in the future. It is good practice for most users to receive at least one home assessment by members of a CMHT.

79. But an analysis of case files revealed that this did not always happen and that, in some areas, people were far more likely to receive at least one-half of their assessments at home than in others [EXHIBIT 16]. In site A, where the use of home assessments was low, there was only one consultant available for a population of 39,000 over the age of 65, so less time was available for her to do home visits.

EXHIBIT 16

The percentage of users receiving home-based assessments

People in some areas were far more likely to receive at least one-half of their assessments at home than in others.

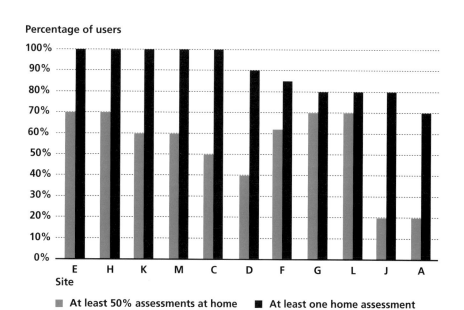

Percentage of users

Site

■ At least 50% assessments at home   ■ At least one home assessment

Source: Audit Commission study of case files

80. In two sites (K and E) the consultants reported that they always saw people at home instead of using outpatient clinics. The use of home assessments was high in these sites [EXHIBIT 16]. Most of these visits were described as 'community clinics' and did not entail extra costs to the GP practice in the way that a formal domiciliary visit would, thus enabling a greater use of home assessment. The GPs' satisfaction with local services was considerably above average in site K and average in site E [EXHIBIT 12, p36]. In contrast, in two of the three sites in which only a few first assessments were carried out at home, GPs' satisfaction with local services was low (sites A and B).

81. Users should receive at least one home assessment by members of a CMHT. Those with complex needs should have further reviews or re-assessments at intervals, when this is appropriate. The use of home assessments that do not entail additional costs to the GP should be encouraged by commissioners as a matter of good practice.

Home care

82. Home care is one of the key services for supporting people at home, if it is provided flexibly and sensitively, to suit the needs of users and carers. It can range from a few hours of help with household tasks per week to intensive personal care. The relationship with the home carer and the quality of the help they provide can make all the difference to older people and their carers. In some sites, home care at weekends and evenings was provided by a different agency than during weekdays. This led to a complicated mix of agencies for some older people and their carers to cope with. One carer described how nine different care workers came into the house during the week for his wife's care. He felt that the most they could have coped with comfortably was three. In addition, he had to contact many different agencies when he wanted to go away for a two-week holiday. Home care at night can enable some people with high needs to remain at home, but it was available in only four sites.

83. Specialist home-care workers for mental health were employed in five sites. These had a number of advantages over non-specialists:

- better understanding of the problems of the users and their carers, and a greater ability to cope with their behaviour;

- greater continuity of care for users as there were fewer workers for them to get to know;

- easier co-ordination between home care, CMHTs and other specialist staff. GPs in these five areas were more likely to agree that services for older people with dementia and depression were satisfactory[I] and that they had ready access to specialist advice than in other areas.[II]

I   Both significant at the .05 level, using Student's t-Test.

II Both significant at the .05 level, using Student's t-Test.

Home care is one of the key services for supporting people at home, if it is provided flexibly and sensitively, to suit the needs of users and carers

84. In site K there was no specialist home-care team for older people with mental health problems, but some informal specialisation. The mental health teams and the local ADS group also provided mental health training for the home carers in their area. Areas without specialist home carers should consider training home-care staff who express an interest in developing skills in this area.

Medication for people on community caseloads

85. The medication that people receive can have a major effect on their well-being, so it is important to get it right. But clinical practice in prescribing medication varies for people with apparently similar conditions. For example, 25 per cent of those with dementia in the community in site B received mood stabilisers (such as Lithium) compared with an average of 8 per cent across all of the sites [EXHIBIT 17A, overleaf]. The use of antipsychotic medication was higher in sites G and J than in any of the others (although the number of cases in site G was small). Antipsychotic medication and anxiolytics are known to lead to problematic side-effects in some older people with dementia, so they should be used sparingly, at the lowest possible effective dose (Refs. 70 and 71).

86. Antidementia drugs have been the subject of considerable debate, mainly about their clinical and cost-effectiveness. The cost of the drugs themselves is comparable with that of other drugs commonly used under the NHS, but the extra monitoring required for someone taking them leads to additional expense. The Standing Medical Advisory Committee has produced guidelines for assessment, supervision and review. The evidence available to date on their effectiveness is mixed. Recent studies have provided positive evidence for the effects of Donepezil (the first antidementia drug to be licensed in the UK) (Ref. 72), even though one review paper has advised that GPs should not continue with any consultant-initiated prescription until more trials have been carried out (Ref. 73). Other studies have noted that the drug can lead to significant improvements, or a slowing down of the decline in functioning, that could imply a reduction in the level of care needed, thus offsetting the increase in medical costs. As any savings would accrue mainly to social care agencies, estimates of the overall cost-benefits of antidementia drugs need to take into account the costs to all agencies. The costs and benefits for older people and their carers should also be taken into account. In the sites where antidementia drugs were available, GPs were more likely to agree that 'there are satisfactory specialised services to meet the need of older people with dementia' than in others.[I] Although new dementia drugs were available in six of the sites, in only one site were they given to more than 10 per cent of people with dementia in the community receiving care from specialist professionals.

I   Significant at the .005 level, using Student's t-Test.

Consultants should be encouraged to review their use of medication in relation to the practices of other consultants, where they are caring for people with similar conditions or needs

87. For those with functional illnesses, antidepressants were the most commonly used group, but the use of antipsychotic and other drugs varied **[EXHIBIT 17B]**. In site J, almost as many people were receiving antipsychotic medication as were receiving antidepressants, which is surprising since depression is much more common than psychosis. Consultants should be encouraged to review their use of medication in relation to the practices of other consultants, where they are caring for people with similar conditions or needs. The National Institute for Clinical Excellence (NICE) is reviewing the evidence on the use of medication for older people with mental health problems, and will produce guidelines. This should help to reduce the variation in local practice. Pharmacists are also an important resource, providing advice on drug treatment to nursing homes and care staff in other settings. Other types of treatment and therapy need to be considered at the same time.

Other community services

88. Some innovative schemes run by voluntary organisations provide essential services that enable people who might otherwise need to use residential care to continue living in their own homes. A housing repair service **[CASE STUDY 6, overleaf]** and a home care service **[CASE STUDY 7, overleaf]** are two such examples. Crossroads is a national voluntary organisation with local branches that provides respite by caring for the user at home or taking them out for short periods. Carers often prefer this to respite care in a residential setting, as it is less disruptive for them and their relative. In site M, a special Crossroads service for older people with mental health problems was funded through the social services' Special Transitional Grant (STG). The service provides respite in the evenings or at weekends as well as during weekdays. The staff receive training in mental healthcare from local mental health professionals and the local ADS branch. Service managers should consider making home-based respite care available in all areas.

EXHIBIT 17

The use of medication for community cases (a) people with dementia and (b) people with functional problems

A

25 per cent of those with dementia in site B received mood stabilisers...

Percentage of users with dementia

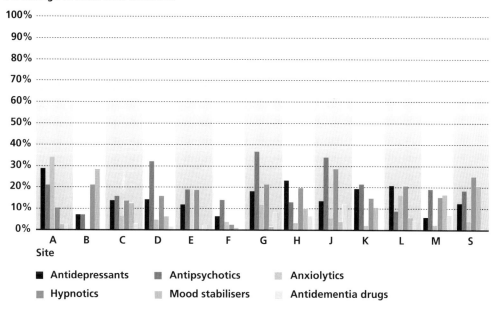

B

...but antidepressants were the most commonly used group of drugs/medication for those with functional illnesses.

Percentage of users with functional mental health problems

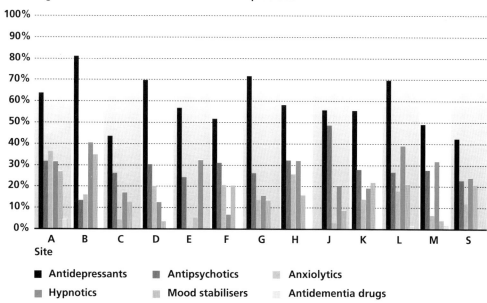

Source: Audit Commission survey of individual case information

CASE STUDY 6

The Bridgend 'Care and Repair' scheme

This scheme has been developed for people at risk, such as those with disabilities or older people with mental health problems. It is managed by a voluntary organisation and jointly funded by social services and the housing department. If someone living in the community has a housing problem such as a leaking roof or a broken front door, the scheme can have it mended within 48 hours. Up to £250 can be spent for each single repair. The scheme has enabled a number of older people with mental health problems to remain in their own homes by making them safe, thus removing the need for admission to residential care. This has been particularly important for older people with mental health problems who would otherwise have felt unsafe staying in their homes. Funding has been agreed for an extension to the scheme, specifically to meet the needs of people with dementia, using technology such as monitors and alarm systems.

CASE STUDY 7

The North Tyneside home sitting service

The local ADS branch provides a care service that enables carers to have a break while their relative is cared for at home, on an individual basis. Older people are helped to engage in activities at home or taken out for a few hours, if this is what they and their carers want. The service is run mainly by volunteers who are co-ordinated by a paid member of staff. It is highly appreciated by the carers who use it.

Outpatient services

Outpatient clinics

89. The use of outpatient clinics can vary, depending partly on consultants' preferences either for seeing people at home or in the clinic [EXHIBIT 18]. The composition of the caseload will also make a difference. In areas with a high rate of functional mental health problems, such as inner cities, more people may attend outpatient clinics. In site F, an inner city area, there is a comparatively high rate of outpatient attendances.

90. In principle, specialist memory clinics should attract people to attend at an earlier stage as they have a more positive public image than a traditional psychiatric service. Memory clinics were provided in five of the 12 study areas. The extent of the provision varied from a permanent base with a team of full-time medical, nursing, psychology and OT staff to a clinic on one half-day per week. In one site, the clinic did not have a base, so the prescription and monitoring of antidementia drugs was always carried out in people's homes. This approach may be preferable,

EXHIBIT 18

Outpatient sessions used per week per 10,000 population over 65

The use of outpatient clinics can vary, depending partly on consultants' preferences.

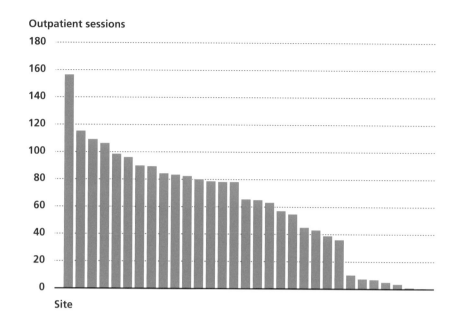

Outpatient sessions

Site

Source: Audit Commission resource mapping survey

as assessment is often more accurate when the person is in his/her own home. Some memory clinics carried out screening tests for physical conditions but others required the GP to do these before a referral would be accepted. Some reviewed progress after a month, but others waited three months. The arrangements depended partly on funding, as some clinics received funding through drug companies or through research money from the health authority or national trials. GPs appeared to value this service, as shown by their greater satisfaction with advice and specialised services for older people with dementia in areas that had a memory clinic than in other areas.[1] There was no difference in GPs' responses to these questions in relation to depression.

91. In one recently established memory clinic, a small local study indicated that around one-half of the 98 people selected to receive Donepezil had improved after three months, as indicated by scores on the MMSE and Alzheimer's Disease Assessment Scale (ADAS, Ref. 74) tests. Some had stopped taking it due to adverse side effects. Those who had not shown measurable improvement after three months were withdrawn from the drug, even though their behaviour and social functioning could have improved in ways that were not identified in the formal tests. It was also possible that they had declined in functioning more slowly than they would have done without the drug.

I   Significant at the .005 level, using Student's t-Test.

92. Where memory clinics are available, their effects and their integration with other services should be monitored and evaluated. This should include an assessment of whether they attract people at an early stage who would not have attended mainstream mental health services for older people. Health and social care commissioners should consider together whether antidementia drugs should be made available locally, taking the potential benefits to all agencies, as well as users and carers, into account. Discussions of future service developments, especially for people in the early stages of dementia, may need to involve local authority representatives, physicians, neurologists and clinical psychologists as much as psychiatrists.

Therapeutic approaches

93. Older people with mental health problems can benefit from a range of group or individual therapies. Some are most useful for specific problems such as depression, anxiety or bereavement, although most people will benefit from social interaction and mental stimulation, including reminiscence.

94. People with depression can be helped by cognitive behavioural therapy (CBT). It helps them to change their typically negative beliefs and assumptions about themselves and the world around, through identifying and testing the validity of such beliefs. It can be effective over the long-term (Ref. 75) and can be undertaken in a relatively short number of sessions (10 to 15). Family therapy can also be helpful as problems often arise from interpersonal difficulties, especially for people with caring responsibilities. Providers of outpatient and day services should make sure that they offer a range of therapies to older people with functional illnesses such as depression, and not simply rely on drug treatments and electro-convulsive therapy (ECT).

95. People with dementia can benefit from reality orientation, reminiscence and validation therapy (Ref. 76). Music therapy, art therapy and other creative therapies can be helpful. Behaviour management approaches that promote understanding of the behaviour of the person with dementia can also be very useful. Most of the research on these approaches has been relatively small scale, with only short periods of follow-up.

96. **Reality orientation**, however, has been shown to improve people's performance if it is carried out in a comprehensive and consistent way. It should be a combination of a constant, 24 hour process in which the environment and every interaction is seen as an opportunity to involve the person in their surroundings and to present relevant information, as well as additional, more intensive sessions in a small group, working to encourage communication with others. The approach needs to be carefully tailored to the needs of the individual to make sure that it is applied sensitively and appropriately.

97. **Reminiscence and life review** can help dementia sufferers to retain a sense of identity when their short-term memory is lost. A range of triggers, such as pictures, music, food and smells, can be used to prompt recall. Staff can learn more about individuals and what is important to them through this, leading to better care planning and closer relationships. It should also be enjoyable in its own right, and has been shown to improve behaviour in nursing home environments (Ref. 77).

98. **Validation therapy** was developed in the 1960s. It requires a professional to accept the user's experience as valid and real, including their memories and feelings. The aim is to stimulate interaction, including non-verbal communication, facilitate understanding of the emotional content, and to enhance trust. There is little research evidence on its impact, but its use has led to a more compassionate approach to understanding and coping with confusion in old age (Ref. 78).

99. **Snoezelen** was developed in Holland. It uses sensory experiences of light and sound, usually in a dark room, and a variety of materials for touching, smelling and tasting. It can provide a way of making contact with people when verbal communication is restricted or no longer possible, and has been shown to have positive effects on the behaviour, mood and cognitive performance of older people with dementia (Ref. 79).

100. Those providing outpatient and day services should ensure that a range of therapies for people with mental health problems are available in all areas. More research should be conducted on the effectiveness of the therapies available and how to implement them effectively, since the context of the building, staffing, facilities and ethos of the setting where they are carried out is likely to be as important as the therapy itself. Therapies also need to be part of an integrated package of care for the individual.

Day provision

101. Day care can be provided by health (day hospitals) or social care agencies (day centres). The use of specialist day services for older people with mental health problems varies [**EXHIBIT 19**]. In many areas, social services cater for some people with mental health needs in their general day provision for older people, as well as providing specialist care. Day hospitals for older people with mental health problems were available in all 12 areas although, in some, the provision was limited to only two days per week or to a small number of places on a ward or in a day hospital for younger people.

102. In nine of the 12 areas, people with dementia were accommodated on different days or in different units from those with functional problems. This is generally accepted as good practice, as the needs of the two groups differ. Those with dementia may have lost the ability to interact socially or intellectually, so they are likely to need more physical and personal care and simpler activities that rely less on memory. But setting aside different days means that people with high needs cannot attend every day, so using a different part of the building may be better in some cases. Providers and commissioners of day care should ensure that individuals with functional illness and dementia receive the most effective care.

EXHIBIT 19

Specialist day care sessions for older people with mental health problems used per week per 10,000 population over 65

The use of specialist day care services for older people with mental health problems varies.

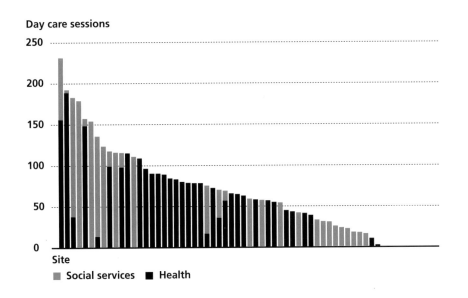

Day care sessions

Note: Day care sessions are defined as half-day sessions. For example, a centre with 10 places occupied five days per week uses 100 sessions.

Source: Audit Commission resource mapping survey

Health and social services agencies need to plan their provision together, to ensure that they make best use of all the available resources

103. NHS day hospitals are better used for time-limited assessment and treatment, while day centres tend to cater for people's longer-term needs. Day centre users are more likely to attend on four or five days per week over a long period of time, compared with one or two days for a shorter period in day hospitals. But the average length of stay in some day hospitals was more than eight years [EXHIBIT 20]. These day hospitals were not being used effectively for the time-limited treatment and assessment of functional and organic mental health problems, despite a stated intention of doing this in all areas. In one-half of the sites, a few people had been attending the day hospital for a year or more. This had arisen because of a lack of long-term day places for people to move on to when their period of assessment or treatment had finished. The consequence for users is that they do not receive appropriate care for their needs and, for providers, that resources are used inefficiently.

104. Health and social services agencies need to plan their provision together, to ensure that they make best use of all the available resources. It is important that the type of provision by one agency facilitates, rather than inhibits, the functioning of the other agencies.

EXHIBIT 20

The average length of stay in day hospitals

The average length of stay in some day hospitals was more than eight years (100 months).

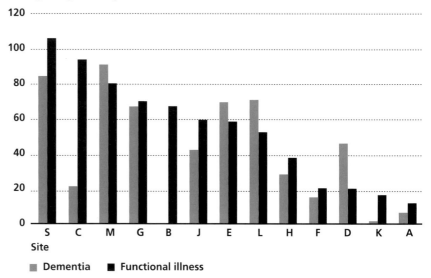

Average length of stay (months)

Site

■ Dementia   ■ Functional illness

Source: Audit Commission survey of individual case information

105. The average level of dependency, as indicated by the CAPE scores, was generally higher in day *centres* than in day *hospitals* [EXHIBIT 21]. This is to be expected if day hospitals are largely used, as intended, for short-term assessment and treatment. People with functional illnesses using day *centres* generally have greater and longer-term needs for support, stimulation and social interaction than those using day *hospitals*. Day *centre* users are more likely to attend on four or five days per week, compared with one or two days in day *hospitals*. In four sites the average level of dependency was very high – equivalent to that expected in residential care – indicating that people are being helped to stay at home. But the type of care depends on which agency manages the building. Many long-term centres are run by voluntary organisations whose staff have limited specialist training, so it is more difficult for them to cope with people who need intensive care. The resources devoted to day provision should be more appropriately matched with the needs of the users. Long-term day support needs to be planned jointly by the local agencies, and should employ the most appropriate mix of staff for the users' needs. This could mean existing facilities and buildings being used flexibly to suit individual needs.

106. In 5 of the 12 sites, some long-term places were funded by the NHS, although the service was managed by a voluntary organisation. In one, the day centres were used by a mix of people, some funded by health and others by social services. There were no observable differences in the level of dependency of the two groups, and staff treated them identically. Some staff members were unaware of the differences in funding. The difference for the users was that the social services group had to pay for their lunch

EXHIBIT 21

Level of dependency of people in day hospitals and day centres

The average level of dependency was generally higher in day centres than in day hospitals.

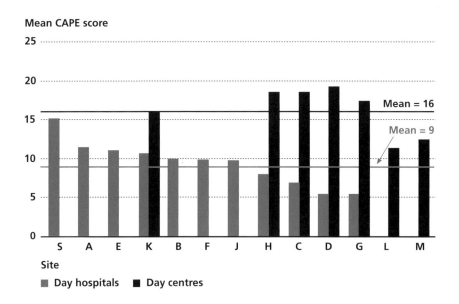

Source: Audit Commission survey of individual case information

and transport, whereas the health-funded group did not. Many of their carers were unhappy about these arrangements. Health and social services agencies should ensure, between them, that users with equivalent needs have equal access to day services and that any charges are based on need rather than on the referral route. One way to achieve this is through pooling budgets to provide integrated day services. Commissioners of services should work collaboratively to develop charging policies based on equity for individuals and that reflect needs.

107. Some people need day care seven days a week, but it is often not available at weekends. Some weekend day care was available in eight of the 12 areas, but in nearly all of these only a small number of places was provided and it was limited to one day. Day care in people's homes was available in four areas, for small numbers of people. In some, this was provided through social services but in others through voluntary organisations such as ADS. A day centre in Islington, however, was providing an intensive service for a group of highly dependent individuals [CASE STUDY 8]. If intensive day care of this kind were available more widely, more people could be helped to live in their own homes for longer, without needing to move into residential care.

108. Very little long-term day care was available for people with functional illness in most sites. Sometimes users could be accommodated in centres for younger people with mental health problems but many found these disturbing and did not feel comfortable there. Commissioners and service managers should ensure that long-term daytime activities for people with functional mental illnesses and dementia are available in all areas. These may not be dependent on specific buildings but might be provided through staff supporting people in other settings.

CASE STUDY 8

Lough Road Day Centre, Islington

The centre is open from 7.30am until 8pm seven days a week and caters for people with advanced dementia. Most of the 21 users attend every day. The extended hours enable carers to continue to work. The staff provide transport in the centre's bus. Since most people are collected and returned home at different times to suit them, there are no delays. Staff receive special training in working with older people with dementia and the consultant visits regularly to talk with them. Respite care is available in a different part of the same building, so the users can continue to spend their day in familiar surroundings with people they know when they are staying overnight. The cost is comparatively high, although cheaper than residential care, at £37 per day, but the service is supporting people in the community who would otherwise be likely to be in residential care or, at least, be receiving an intensive package of home care. The average CAPE score at the centre was 19, compared to an average of 17 in day centres nationally.

In some areas, it was not uncommon for people to spend over two hours in an ambulance before reaching the day hospital

Transport

109. Enabling people to get to and from day provision was a problem in most of the sites. Where an ambulance was used to bring people to the day hospital, users almost always experienced long delays on the journey while other users were picked up. In some areas, it was not uncommon for people to spend over two hours in an ambulance before reaching the day hospital. This can be stressful and uncomfortable, especially for people who are confused or physically frail. It also meant that the day's programme might not begin until after 11.00am and might finish before 3.00pm. Sometimes group activities had to start at different times, depending on which people arrived first, so running a programme of structured groups was difficult. These were the disadvantages of using a dedicated ambulance, and had to be weighed up with the advantages, in some areas, of having a trained ambulance crew who could check up on people if they did not come to the door as expected.

110. Some services use local taxis, which are more efficient and also cheaper. Sometimes it is possible for the taxi service to use regular drivers who get to know the individuals and report back if any problems arise. Other services use volunteer drivers who are trained in working with people with mental health problems, but the availability of sufficient, reliable volunteers in the local area varies. In others, a local 'dial-a-ride' service can be used. Commissioners and providers of day services should monitor the effects of the transport they use and, if there are problems, consider changing to a more flexible arrangement, such as a local taxi service.

Special needs

111. Younger people with dementia are often accommodated in day provision for older people. This can be unhelpful for them, as their needs are likely to be different, unless they have highly individualised activity programmes. Many are physically fit and able. Their families are also likely to need additional support and counselling, as they may have particular difficulty in dealing with their situation. A special project in site J, funded through the Mental Illness Specific Grant (MISG), provides joint health and social services day care, one day per week. In the first month, 19 referrals were received, indicating a high level of previously unmet need. In site K, a specialist day service for younger people with dementia is provided two days per week by the local ADS. One of these days is jointly funded by the NHS trust. At least one mental health professional should have a designated responsibility for younger people with dementia in all areas.

112. Older people from minority ethnic groups need special consideration, to ensure that appropriate services are provided for them. This does not necessarily mean special services, but usually requires some change to the existing provision. Some culturally appropriate services were provided in 5 of the 12 sites. In three, there were specialist day centres for either African-Caribbean older people or for some South Asian groups, but these were not unique to mental health. In site L, some of the medical staff had skills in a range of Asian languages. User groups from ethnic minorities generally say that they prefer not to be given separate day care services, but for the mainstream services to be sensitive to their needs. This would not only include appropriate food, but arrangements for their religious practices and staff who can speak a language that they can understand.

113. People living in rural areas, such as parts of Wales, can have difficulty in getting access to day services. Even if transport were available, it would take too long for some of them to travel to a day centre in a main town. Travelling day care is available in some areas, for example, Daybreak in Nottinghamshire [CASE STUDY 9].

CASE STUDY 9

Daybreak, Nottinghamshire

This is a day service managed jointly by health and social services, funded by MISG and Nottinghamshire social services. It operates in a rural borough within Nottinghamshire, on three different days of the week, taking 12 users per day. Existing community centres in villages are used for the day centres. These have the advantage of being familiar to the users and their families and not being associated with mental health. Additional equipment is brought in a van with the staff of the service, so a range of activities for physical and mental stimulation are available. The programme includes frequent outings to places nearby.

Respite care

114. Respite care, to give carers a break, is essential to enable them to continue caring. It was mentioned more often by carers in the Audit Commission survey than any other service.

'I would like more time and space to myself.'

'... affordable respite care...'

'...occasional relief for carer...'

'I should like a sitting service with more flexibility for afternoon or night time.'

'Easy access to respite care at weekends.'

'Perhaps someone to sit while I get out by myself.'

(Audit Commission survey)

Respite care is usually provided in residential or hospital settings, but in 3 of the 12 study sites it was available at home. Some respite care beds were available in all 12 study sites but the number of places available varied [EXHIBIT 22]. Less than one-half of the 850 carers surveyed said that they could get access to as much respite care as they needed. Hospital-based respite care is usually reserved for those with severe behavioural problems or additional needs for physical care. But in two sites there was no provision for respite care in hospital and in four others it depended on the pressure on acute beds. Carers could book a respite placement on the understanding that it might have to be cancelled if the ward filled up with people needing emergency admission. In some others, respite was provided on continuing care wards, in which a number of places were kept permanently available. The availability of NHS continuing care beds varies locally from none at all to 32 per 10,000 people over the age of 65 (see para. 148). Health commissioners and providers should ensure that some hospital provision for respite care is available in all areas.

EXHIBIT 22

Respite beds used per week by health and social services per 10,000 population over 65

The number of places available varies.

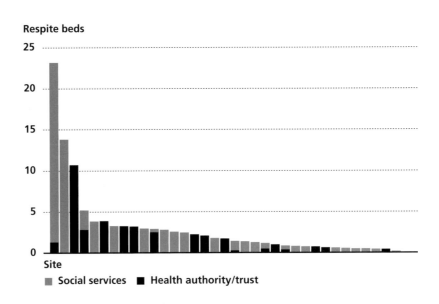

Source: Audit Commission resource mapping survey

In some sites, carers were able to book respite care directly with the manager of the home or ward

115. In all 12 areas, some respite places were provided in residential and nursing homes, funded by social services, with contributions from the user or carer. Many carers feel that they should not have to pay for this. Some carers who responded to the survey commented:

'The more help you get the more you pay.'

'It all depends on whether the client has savings and of course the magical figure is £16,000 above which you pay for everything. £10,000 or less and you have no worries.'

'My wife is now in a nursing home of my choice at my expense.'
(Audit Commission survey)

116. The Royal Commission on Long Term Care has recommended that personal care be free to users, although this would run contrary to much of the current Government policy to promote personal responsibility (through stakeholder pensions, for example). Some commentators have also noted that such a change would give older people less opportunity to have the dignity of choosing the type of care they want for themselves and, by stretching resources, could lower the quality of care (Ref. 80). Suggested alternatives include a range of insurance and loan schemes that could defer the disposal of assets until someone dies (Ref. 81).

117. Some homes will only take individuals for respite care if they happen to have a vacancy, but will not keep places permanently available. This is understandable, since full-time residents provide a more stable income and managers want to avoid having vacant places. So, some social services departments agree to pay continuously for a given number of respite places, whether or not they are filled. This leads to a more predictable situation for both home managers, who have a guaranteed income, and social services care managers, who can arrange placements several months ahead. In some sites, carers were able to book respite care directly with the manager of the home or ward, once they had been accepted as users of the service, without having to make the request through a care manager on each occasion. This made it easier for both carers and the home managers to plan ahead for the days or weeks that they wanted. Social services should reserve and pay for a number of places for respite care in residential or nursing homes on a continuous basis.

118. In addition to planned respite care, emergency respite care is sometimes needed if problems arise at home, such as the carer becoming ill. Occasionally this was available in a residential or nursing home, where one or more of the respite places was reserved for this purpose. More often it was only available in hospital, which may not be appropriate for all users. In one site there were flexible arrangements between health and social services for respite care. If someone needed respite at short notice, the joint health and social services team, who shared an office, discussed the case and made arrangements. Accommodation could be provided in the most suitable place available. This did not require a formal referral from one agency to another as team members worked closely together and saw each other several times a day.

The audits will provide comparative information about the number of places per 10,000 people over 65 available in different areas, which should help with planning

119. Providing respite care in other people's permanent homes is not ideal, unless it is used as a well-managed opportunity for individuals to prepare for a long-term placement. It can be upsetting for those who live there to have new people appearing every week, especially if they have behaviour problems. So, some authorities are developing specific provision for respite care, either in-house or in conjunction with an independent provider. The quality of the environment and the care provided by staff are crucial considerations in the provision of respite care. Managers of respite provision should consult carers about individual needs and ensure that the period of respite does not increase the user's dependency or reduce their well-being. Respite care at home, sometimes for shorter periods, such as a few hours in the evening, may be more appropriate for some users and carers.

120. Health and social services should, between them, ensure that sufficient places for respite care are available, with some reserved for emergency situations. The audits will provide comparative information about the number of places per 10,000 people over 65 available in different areas, which should help with planning. They should aim to provide a range of options, including respite care at home. Non-emergency places may be booked most efficiently by allowing the carer to negotiate directly with the manager of the service.

RECOMMENDATIONS

3 — Services to Help People at Home

Improving home-based services

1   Authorities and trusts should review together the mix of staff they deploy and re-balance where necessary.

2   Service managers should monitor caseloads and the dependency of people supported by CMHTs. This is one of the ways in which commissioners and providers can determine whether their service aims, such as supporting highly dependent individuals at home, are being achieved.

3   Users should receive at least one home assessment by members of a CMHT. Those with complex needs should have further reviews or re-assessments at intervals, when this is appropriate. The use of home assessments that do not entail additional costs to the GP should be encouraged by commissioners as a matter of good practice.

4   Areas without specialist home carers should consider training home-care staff who express interest in developing skills in this area.

5   Consultants should be encouraged to review their use of medication, in relation to the practices of other consultants, where they are caring for people with similar conditions or needs.

6   Service managers should consider making home-based respite care available in all areas.

Offering appropriate outpatient treatment

7   Where memory clinics are available, their effects should be monitored and evaluated. This should include an assessment of whether they attract people at an early stage who would not have attended mainstream mental health services for older people. Health and social care commissioners should consider together whether antidementia drugs should be made available locally, taking the potential benefits to all agencies, as well as users and carers, into account.

8   Providers of outpatient and day services should make sure that they offer a range of therapies to older people with functional illnesses such as depression, and not simply rely on drug treatments and electro-convulsive therapy (ECT).

9   Those providing outpatient and day services should ensure that a range of therapies for people with mental health problems are available in all areas. More research should be conducted on the effectiveness of the therapies available and how to implement them effectively.

3 Services to Help People at Home

Day care to meet individual needs

10 Providers and commissioners of day care should ensure that individuals with functional illness and dementia receive the most effective care. This may be helped by either using different days or different parts of a building.

11 Health and social services need to plan together, to ensure that they make best use of all the available resources. It is important that the type of provision by one agency facilitates, rather than inhibits, the functioning of the other agencies.

12 The resources devoted to day provision should be more appropriately matched with the needs of the users. Long-term day support needs to be planned jointly by the local agencies, and should employ the most appropriate mix of staff for the users' needs. This could mean that existing facilities and buildings are used flexibly to suit individual needs, rather than the type of care depending on which agency manages the building.

13 Health and social services should ensure, between them, that users with equivalent needs have equal access to day services and that any charges are based on need rather than the referral route. One way to achieve this is through pooling budgets to provide integrated day services. Commissioners of services should work collaboratively to develop charging policies that are based on equity for individuals and that reflect needs.

14 Commissioners and service managers should ensure that long-term daytime activities for people with functional mental illnesses and dementia are available in all areas. These may not be dependent on specific buildings but might be provided through staff supporting people in other settings.

15 Day hospitals should, ideally, be used for time-limited assessment and treatment. Commissioners and providers of day services should monitor the effects of the transport they use and, if there are problems, consider changing to a more flexible arrangement, such as a local taxi service.

16 At least one mental health professional should have a designated responsibility for younger people with dementia in all areas.

RECOMMENDATIONS

3 ___ Services to Help People at Home

Providing respite when it is needed

17 Health commissioners and providers should ensure that some hospital provision is available in all areas for respite care.

18 Social services should reserve and pay for a number of places for respite care in residential or nursing homes on a continuous basis.

19 Health and social services should, between them, ensure that sufficient places for respite care are available, some of which should be reserved for emergency situations. Non-emergency places may be booked most efficiently by allowing the carer to negotiate directly with the manager of the service. They should aim to provide a range of high-quality options, including respite care at home.

20 Managers of residential respite provision should consult carers about individual needs and ensure that the period of respite does not increase the user's dependency or reduce their well-being.

4 ——

Hospital and Residential Provision

Some people need a spell in hospital to treat a psychiatric or
behaviour problem, but the provision and use of hospital beds
varies, especially for people with dementia. Some admissions
might be avoided if residential and nursing homes were
supported by specialist mental health professionals. The cost
and quality of care in residential and nursing homes varies.
Training staff in techniques such as 'dementia care
mapping' (DCM) can be helpful.

Acute psychiatric wards

121. When people's problems are severe, they may need a spell in hospital to help stabilise their behaviour. However, people with dementia were more likely to be admitted to hospital in some areas than in others. Some consultants try to resist making an admission if possible, feeling that the stress of a hospital admission might increase the person's disorientation, so they prefer to undertake comprehensive assessments in community settings, in conjunction with colleagues of other disciplines. Their home visits might be supplemented by a few days at the day hospital where physical tests could be carried out. Other consultants felt that most people with dementia should be admitted to hospital for a week or so as part of their routine assessment. Sometimes divergent views on this matter were held by different consultants within the same trust. As a consequence, the number of beds used and the number of admissions for people with dementia varied considerably between trusts [EXHIBIT 23]. Sites with highly developed community services tended to make less use of hospital admissions. The CAPE score, indicating the average level of dependency, also varied [EXHIBIT 24, overleaf]. A high average level of dependency on the ward implies that fewer people with dementia are admitted to hospital and greater use is made of community services.

122. Ideally, admission should only be necessary to stabilise behaviour problems that are unmanageable in any other setting or to treat any severe psychiatric symptoms. Where the dependency of people with dementia on acute psychiatric wards is low, commissioners and local professionals should review their practices to see whether some of those admitted could be more appropriately assessed and cared for in community settings.

EXHIBIT 23

Acute psychiatric beds occupied by people with dementia per 10,000 population over 65

The number of beds occupied by people with dementia varied considerably.

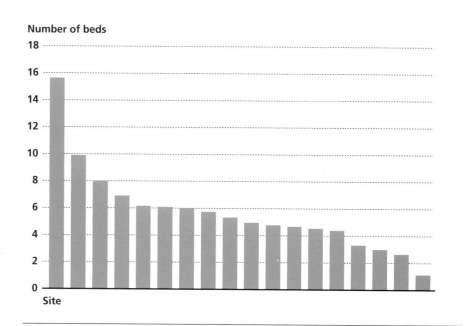

Number of beds

Source: Audit Commission resource mapping survey

EXHIBIT 24

Mean CAPE score for people with dementia on acute psychiatric wards

A high average level of dependency on the ward implies that fewer people with dementia are admitted to hospital.

Mean CAPE score

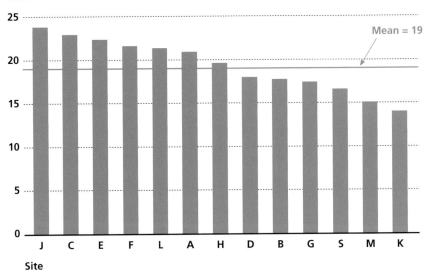

Source: Audit Commission survey of individual case information

123. Most older people are admitted to psychiatric wards from their own homes but some come from other settings, such as other hospital wards or residential or nursing homes **[EXHIBIT 25]**. The decision to transfer someone usually arises when their behaviour causes problems that cannot be managed where they are. In site E, almost one-quarter of the people admitted to old age psychiatry wards had been transferred from other hospital wards. Close links between mental health services and physical health services for older people are essential, because so many users have both kinds of need. Many are admitted for a physical problem that can be complicated by their mental health needs. Although some transfers of people who initially came into hospital for physical care are necessary, a very high number implies that relationships between the services may be poor. Where professionals working in acute or geriatric services do not have sufficient knowledge of mental health care, they may choose to transfer people at the first indication of a mental health problem. It is important that some staff in generic settings have specialist knowledge and skills in the assessment and management of those with mental health problems. Specialists in mental health and physical care for older people should ensure that they communicate with each other and provide support and training when it is needed. Visits by medical and nursing staff to patients on other wards and the provision of support and advice should minimise the need for such transfers. Regular liaison meetings and case conferences may facilitate this. Jointly managed assessment units, which can reduce the need for transfers, operate in some areas.

EXHIBIT 25

Previous accommodation of people on acute psychiatric wards – the average for all sites and in two contrasting sites

In site E, almost one-quarter of the people admitted to old age psychiatry wards had been transferred from other hospital wards.

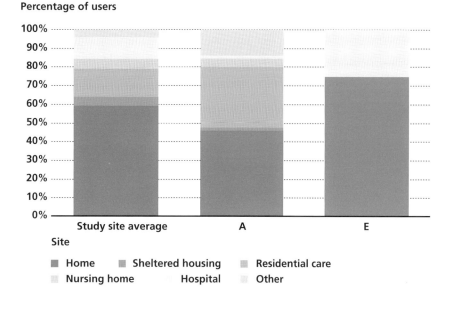

Percentage of users

Site

- Home
- Sheltered housing
- Residential care
- Nursing home
- Hospital
- Other

Source: Audit Commission survey of individual case information

124. Ideally, some mental health beds should be based on the same site as a general hospital, but if staff visit each other and communicate frequently, the difficulties of being physically separate can be overcome. Ensuring that they communicate effectively is more important than the organisational structures, and changes to these should be minimised.

125. In site A, 33 per cent of the people on acute wards had been admitted from residential homes, compared with an average of 14 per cent in other sites [EXHIBIT 25]. This could have been due to staff in these homes not having sufficient specialist skills in mental health care to manage the behaviour of these individuals. Some of these admissions might have been avoided if specialist professionals from the mental health services had provided support and training for the staff of the residential homes. Support for residential staff caring for people with mental health problems was available in only four of the 12 sites. The managers of many homes expressed a wish for more frequent contact with old age psychiatrists. Old age psychiatrists and community teams should provide support to residential homes that care for large numbers of people with mental health problems. This may help to avoid some hospital admissions and to improve the quality of life for residents.

126. It is generally accepted to be good practice to provide separate areas for people with dementia and for those with functional illnesses on acute psychiatric wards. People with severe depression, for example, may find that sharing their living space with other people with behaviour

NATIONAL REPORT • FORGET ME NOT

problems can make them feel worse. The effect on people with dementia of sharing a ward with severely depressed people may also be unhelpful. The type of supervision needed for the two groups may be quite different. Separate areas were provided in 9 of the 12 sites but the 2 groups were accommodated together in some wards in 3 others. Providers should aim to make separate living spaces available on wards for those with dementia and those with functional mental illnesses. An appropriate physical environment includes sufficient space for people to walk around safely, a high proportion of single rooms, facilities for those with physical or sensory disabilities, somewhere quiet for relatives to meet with users, privacy for bathing and the availability of stimulating activities and facilities such as chiropody, dental care and hairdressing.

127. Although most people with dementia were admitted to hospital as voluntary patients, in two sites around one-half had been admitted compulsorily under a section of the Mental Health Act 1983. This reflects a national increase in the number of compulsory admissions between October 1997 and June 1998, following a ruling by the Court of Appeal on a case commonly referred to as the 'Bournewood Case'. The ruling had stated that the informal admission and treatment of a compliant 'incapacitated' patient was unlawful, but the decision was later overturned by the House of Lords. Nevertheless, the case has raised awareness among those responsible for admissions to hospital and has emphasised the need to ensure that procedures concerning patients' rights are fully complied with. This is especially important where an individual's ability to make decisions is in doubt. It is good practice for such patients to be visited periodically by the hospital managers or an independent advocate if no one from outside the hospital is taking a continuing interest in their care (Ref. 82).

128. People are usually admitted to hospital to stabilise a psychiatric or behaviour problem, so they should not normally stay longer than 6–8 weeks. Many should stay for a much shorter period – a week or so – and the maximum should be about three months. But the length of time that people with dementia stay on acute psychiatric wards varies [EXHIBIT 26]. In areas where they generally stay longer than three months, there may be difficulty in arranging placements in residential or nursing homes, either because of a lack of suitable places or because social services cannot arrange the funding. In some areas this delayed discharge has led to 'bed blocking', where insufficient acute beds are available when needed. Most of the delayed discharges for older people are for people with dementia, as more of them are admitted to residential and nursing homes than those with functional illnesses. Health and social services should share information and plan together for long-term care, to enable people to be cared for in the most appropriate setting. Pooled budgets that enable a more flexible use of health and social care resources can help to achieve this.

EXHIBIT 26

Mean length of stay on acute psychiatric wards for people with dementia

Where the average stay is longer than three months, there may be difficulty in arranging placements in residential or nursing homes.

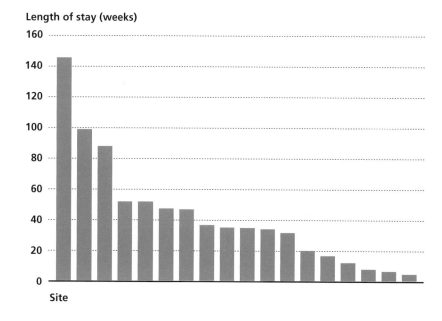

Length of stay (weeks)

Site

Source: Audit Commission resource mapping survey

Long-term accommodation and care

High-care sheltered housing

129. Older people sometimes choose to move into sheltered housing – especially designed units with warden support. It is possible to receive extra care in some of these developments. This is also known as 'very sheltered housing', and was available to older people with mental health problems in 3 of the 12 sites, usually within an ordinary sheltered housing complex. Arrangements were made with social services for the provision of intensive home care, in addition to the support from on-site staff, meals and communal activities that were available to all tenants.

130. For many people with functional mental health problems, these arrangements can provide a good balance of independence, privacy and dignity, with sufficient support when needed. It may also suit people with mild or moderate dementia if they have moved to sheltered accommodation before their dementia became significant. But those who move to their flat after the dementia has begun to be pronounced can experience difficulty in adapting to the physical and social environment. They have to spend a considerable amount of time alone, which can be distressing for people who are confused and whose sense of time has been lost. Meeting their needs adequately would require either most of the day spent in communal areas with others (thus removing much of the advantage of having one's own flat) or an individual carer being present for virtually all of their waking hours – which would be very costly.

Less than one-half of the carers surveyed said that they knew of a residential or nursing home that provided good quality care or how to explore the possibility of a place for their relative

Residential and nursing home care

131. The decision to move into residential or nursing home care is one of the most significant taken by users of services or their carers and has the greatest cost implications [EXHIBIT 3, p19]. A number of viewpoints should be taken into account, especially the carer and/or user, as well as others who have been involved in their care. In some sites, staff reported that decisions were made mainly by the consultant and it was difficult for anyone to disagree, even though the funding was provided by social services. In others, a social services 'panel' including a range of professionals, such as CPNs and medical staff, contribute relevant information to support the decision. However, different practices occur under the title of 'panel'. In some areas it can be a cost-driven local authority requirement, in which few of the professionals with specialist knowledge are involved. Some groups may be reluctant to share information, for reasons of confidentiality, although this can usually be overcome if relationships between the agencies are good. The General Medical Council has provided some useful guidance on confidentiality and information sharing (Ref. 83).

132. Carers need to be given good information about the options for residential and nursing home care in their area. Less than one-half of the carers surveyed said that they knew of a residential or nursing home that provided good quality care or how to explore the possibility of a place for their relative. Social services should aim to take into account the views of a range of professionals, as well as users and carers, in decisions to admit people to residential or nursing home care, to ensure that the services provided meet the needs of the user.

133. Of those in residential homes, three-quarters enter from their own homes, compared with only around one-fifth of those admitted to nursing homes. Of those in specialist mental health nursing homes, one-third were admitted from other nursing or residential homes, implying that those homes were unable to cope [EXHIBIT 27]. Better support for residential and nursing homes by specialist mental health professionals could help to reduce the number of such moves, which can be detrimental to the health and well-being of the residents. Sometimes residential and nursing care can be provided on a single site, enabling people to receive more intensive care when they need it without having to experience a change of location or care regime. Commissioners of health and social care should monitor the number of moves from residential and nursing homes to other residential settings and use this as one indicator of the quality of care provided.

EXHIBIT 27

Previous accommodation of residents of nursing homes

Of those in specialist mental health nursing homes, one-third were admitted from other nursing or residential homes.

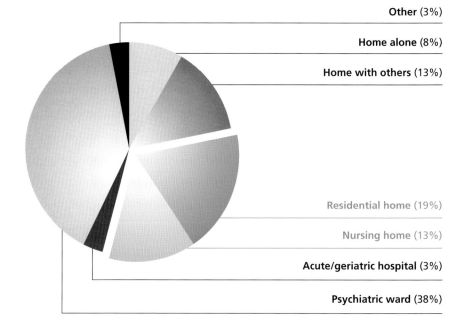

Other (3%)

Home alone (8%)

Home with others (13%)

Residential home (19%)

Nursing home (13%)

Acute/geriatric hospital (3%)

Psychiatric ward (38%)

Source: Audit Commission survey of individual case information

134. Some homes specialise in the care of people with dementia. These people do not necessarily need qualified nurses to look after them unless they have additional physical or mental health needs, but they do need staff who are trained to meet their special needs in order for them to receive quality care. Although specialist residential care is not a separate legal category for the purposes of registration, many local authorities have made arrangements to recognise this specialisation and to pay a higher rate than for ordinary residential homes (usually between the rate for ordinary residential and nursing home care). It can be cost-effective and of a high quality if it is well managed and supported. The extra income makes higher staff ratios and special training possible. In some local authorities, the homes that remain 'in-house' provide specialist care, while ordinary residential care is purchased from the independent sector. In other areas, the local authority is encouraging certain providers to register some homes as specialist, and to develop closer working relationships with them. Some mental health training will be needed in all residential homes, however, as they are all likely to be caring for some people with dementia. Homes with dual nursing and residential care registration can often provide flexible levels of nursing input.

135. Specialist mental health nursing homes can be registered as a legally separate category from other nursing homes, and are required to have a qualified mental health nurse on duty at all times. They usually attract a higher weekly rate than other nursing homes. Specialist residential care for older people with mental health problems was available in 11 of the 12 sites and specialist nursing home care in all of them, but the number of places varied [EXHIBIT 28]. Commissioners need to ensure that sufficient places are available to enable people to leave hospital when they are ready, but not so many that funds are diverted away from services to support people at home.

136. Sometimes special units within ordinary residential homes are set aside for people with mental health problems. These can operate independently with their own staff, but share facilities such as the kitchen and laundry, as well as having extra back-up available if it is needed. Users and their carers may find the image portrayed by these more acceptable to them than homes that are solely for those with mental health problems. In site F, one residential home specialised in the care of older people with functional mental health problems.

137. Monitoring the quality of care provided in residential and nursing homes is essential. Registration and contracting arrangements require a certain level of monitoring, much of it concerned with the physical environment. However, in some areas, attempts were made to monitor the quality of personal care, and to pay providers accordingly. In one site, a 'quality premium' was payable for placements in homes that were deemed

EXHIBIT 28

The number of occupied places in specialist residential and nursing homes per 10,000 population over 65

The number of places used varied.

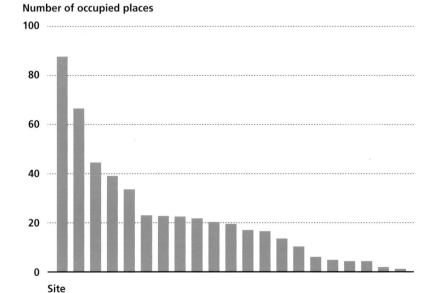

Source: Audit Commission resource mapping survey

to be of a high quality, according to standards established by the social services department, in conjunction with others. The standards covered staff training, staff morale, the physical environment, the quality of care and management arrangements, although none of them was specific to mental health care. Social workers, the local carers' federation and the staff of the homes made independent quality assessments.

138. Quality monitoring of this kind generally only applies to residents who are funded by social services. Nationally, 80 per cent of older people with mental health problems in residential homes and 74 per cent of those in nursing homes are funded by social services. Most of the others pay for the care themselves, but some are supported by a combination of NHS and other sources. Social services should monitor the quality of the care provided in residential and nursing homes, including taking the views of users and/or carers into account. They should also consider paying higher rates for higher quality provision.

139. The level of dependency of people in specialist residential and nursing home care varies [EXHIBIT 29]. In areas where the average dependency in residential homes is low, such as site J, the commissioning agencies should consider whether some people admitted to these homes could be more appropriately supported in the community. In site E, the average dependency in nursing homes was low, implying that some of the residents might be more appropriately supported in residential care. Information on the level of dependency, such as CAPE scores, should be used in strategic decision-making about the levels of residential and nursing home provision in the area.

EXHIBIT 29

The average dependency (CAPE scores) in specialist residential and nursing homes

Where the average dependency is low, commissioning agencies should consider whether some people could be more appropriately supported in the community.

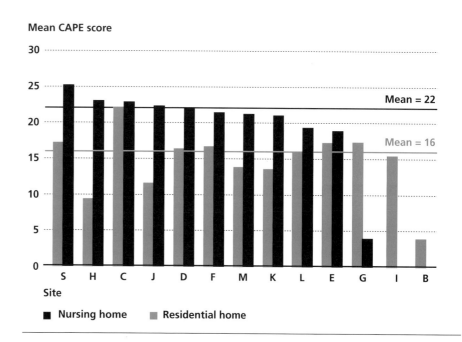

Mean CAPE score

Source: Audit Commission survey of individual case information

140. Social services should encourage providers in their area to develop specialist residential care for older people with dementia, and should be prepared to fund places at a higher rate to reflect the specialist skills needed. The dependency of people placed in residential and nursing homes should be monitored, to ensure that care is provided for them in the most appropriate setting. In conjunction with health and other interest groups, they should monitor the quality of the care provided. This should be part of any best value review in the local authority. The new opportunities for health and social services to pool budgets should also facilitate effective monitoring.

141. When people enter residential or nursing home care, their progress needs to be monitored to make sure the placement is appropriate and that their needs are being met, but formal reviews of progress took place in only one-half of the study sites. Reviews should continue for at least three to six months, to find out how the placement is working out and to provide support, advice and guidance to the staff. This is particularly important where someone is placed in a setting that is not specialised for mental health.

142. Appropriate support, advice and training for staff working in these homes could enable them to cope with difficult behaviour if it occurs, and reduce some admissions to hospital or transfers to other nursing homes. This was provided routinely in only 4 of the 12 sites. In site L, one of the medical staff had a specific responsibility for supporting residential and nursing homes. She routinely visited homes where significant numbers of people had been placed, carrying out home-based reviews and giving staff the opportunity to discuss any difficulties that might have arisen. Consultants and other professionals in the specialist mental health services should provide support to homes in the local area, especially where individuals in their care have been placed in them. Primary health care professionals often become closely involved with residential and nursing homes, so their contribution needs to be co-ordinated with specialist mental health and local authority services.

143. Sometimes the residents of residential and nursing homes may not be receiving the best possible medication for their needs. The use of drugs varied considerably [EXHIBIT 30]. Over one-half of the residents with dementia in site D were receiving hypnotics and anxiolytics, compared with less than one-quarter in most of the other sites. Antipsychotic drugs were given to around two-thirds of residents with dementia in sites J and G. This could mean that, in these homes, drugs rather than staff skills were being used to control behaviour. Antipsychotic medication can help to reduce some symptoms, such as delusions and hallucinations, but they do not remove behaviour problems, such as unsociability, aggression, agitation and poor self care (Ref. 70). They are particularly likely to lead to problematic side-effects in older people with dementia, such as a worsening of cognitive functioning, rigidity and odd involuntary movements, and can be particularly harmful for those with Lewy Body dementia (Refs. 71 and 84). Good practice would imply that only a small minority of residents with dementia receive antipsychotic medication, at the lowest possible effective dose, following a careful assessment. The effects should be closely monitored for benefits and adverse effects. Anxiolytics, such as Diazepam, should also be used very sparingly as they can lead to disinhibition and can increase disorientation and memory problems. In contrast, only around 20 per cent of residents were receiving antidepressant medication, varying from around 5 per cent in site G to 30 per cent in site K. This is despite the fact that around 40 per cent are likely to be suffering from depression (Ref. 28). Residents should be assessed to see whether they are suffering from depression, and treated appropriately with medication or other therapies. Medication for all residents of nursing and residential homes should be reviewed regularly.

EXHIBIT 30

Drugs given to users with dementia in residential and nursing homes

Antipsychotic drugs were given to around two-thirds of residents in sites J and G.

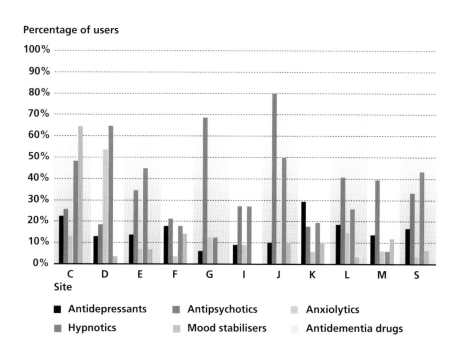

Percentage of users

Source: Audit Commission survey of individual case information

144. Different homes can provide environments of very different qualities. The quality of care provided by the staff is the most important factor, but the physical environment also makes a difference. An appropriate physical environment should include having space for people to walk around safely, personal cues such as colour-coded doors to help people to identify rooms, single bedrooms that people can use when they wish, facilities for those with physical or sensory disabilities, somewhere quiet for relatives to meet with residents, privacy for bathing, and the availability of facilities such as chiropody, dental care and hairdressing. Decoration of the unit should be homely and welcoming. Space for therapeutic and other activities and a garden are also important. Ideally, residents should live in groups of 12 or less – ideally as few as 8 living together if this is possible with the funding available. Residents should be encouraged to bring their own furnishings and belongings. Providing a variety of appropriate and stimulating activities is also important.

145. Dementia care mapping (DCM) was being used in a limited number of settings in 4 of the 12 sites. DCM, for monitoring the environment experienced by users, can make a great deal of difference to the quality of care [BOX B] (Ref. 85). Learning to undertake DCM and getting feedback from it can greatly enhance the awareness and understanding of staff to improve the care they provide. Visits from specialists to monitor the quality of care and support staff can be beneficial for both users and care staff.

146. One specialist residential home, Mayfields, is run by Methodist Homes and provides a high-quality environment for people with severe dementia [CASE STUDY 10]. The Dementia Care Initiative provides high-quality accommodation and support for people with severe dementia in ordinary houses in the community [CASE STUDY 11].

BOX B

Dementia care mapping (DCM)

- Observers spend sessions of three to six hours with a resident.
- They participate but observe during each five-minute period, and make a judgement about the resident's well-being.
- They note any personal 'detractions' that occur (such as the resident being ignored) and their severity.
- Five or six residents can be observed at a time (by an experienced observer).
- Managers receive detailed information about the actions of staff and the interactions that take place in the home.

CASE STUDY 10

Mayfields, Wirral

The residential home is run and staffed by the charity, Methodist Homes for the Aged. It was purpose built to standards approved by the Dementia Services Development Centre at Stirling. Three groups of 12 residents each live on separate wings with their own staff, but are free to move around the whole building. Each wing is decorated a different colour, with differently coloured doors for toilets, bathrooms, kitchens and bedrooms. Each group of 12 is supported by 2 full-time care staff, a general assistant and a domestic, as well as a senior care staff member, a manager and ancillary staff for the home as a whole. The home can manage older people with behavioural problems, but if someone becomes physically ill and needs highly specialised nursing care, such as a drip, they would have to receive that elsewhere. Local volunteers also participate in activities with residents. All staff receive some residential training and placements in other homes, and can take NVQ level 2/3 qualifications. Staff training and support are fundamental to the regime of the home, in which re-learning and maintaining living skills is emphasised at all times. Residents are encouraged with the support of staff to participate in daily living skills – such as baking, ironing, hoovering, dusting, making tea etc – that they have used throughout their lives. DCM is carried out regularly by the manager and deputy.

The weekly cost is £346, of which a significant proportion may be funded by social services.

CASE STUDY 11

Dementia Care Initiative, Newcastle

In this scheme, which is managed by a voluntary organisation, individuals with severe dementia are tenants in ordinary houses owned by the city council or a housing association. All have relatives who did not wish them to go into residential or nursing home care. In a typical house, four tenants are supported by two staff during the day and one member of staff at night. Tenants are encouraged to participate in housework, gardening, shopping and cooking, as far as possible. All of them come from the local area, and family members are likely to drop in at any time. The staff acknowledge that they are guests in the home, and the tenants are encouraged to maintain as much independence as possible. One tenant had a recent spell of four weeks in hospital while she was disturbed and hallucinating, before returning to the house.

The housing and care are paid for by the social services care management budget, together with individual allowances (such as Attendance Allowance) and housing benefit. Twenty-one people with dementia are supported in staffed houses and a further 140 in their own homes. The Dementia Care Initiative also supports three younger people with very severe dementia in a house with three members of staff during the day. The funding for the additional staff comes from the Independent Living Fund, to which younger people are entitled.

Continuing NHS care

147. Those who are most dependent may need long-term or 'continuing' care by the NHS. An expert-group consensus concluded that individuals who need NHS continuing care would be likely to have:

- sustained or frequently difficult behaviour;
- associated physical illness and sensory impairments, with the individual's needs not being able to be better met elsewhere; or
- failure to cope, or more rapid deterioration in other care settings (Ref. 86).

148. The amount needed is the subject of heated debate and its availability varies widely – from none to 32 places per 10,000 people over 65 in the study sites **[EXHIBIT 31]**. Part of the variation is due to the number of 'old long-stay' residents of large hospitals, who will continue to need care for the rest of their lives. In some areas there are many such people, but in others all of the former residents have been resettled elsewhere. However, different policies for continuing care in different health authorities also contribute to the variation. Some have a policy of not funding any continuing care themselves, expecting social services to fund all long-term placements. Others have developed new continuing care provision for people with difficult behaviour or physical frailty. The eligibility criteria vary locally. Commissioners and service managers in one site agreed that people who needed regular weekly monitoring by a psychiatrist should receive continuing NHS care.

EXHIBIT 31

The number of NHS continuing care places per 10,000 population over 65

The availability of NHS-funded continuing care varies widely.

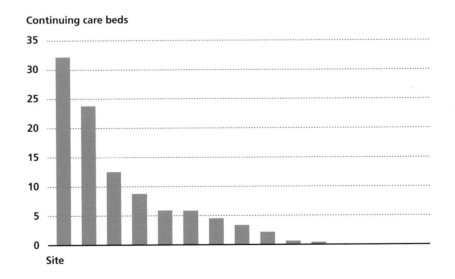

Source: Audit Commission resource mapping survey

*NHS staff could provide
input to nursing homes
on a flexible basis,
depending on the
current needs*

149. The financial arrangements for continuing care also varied. In some areas continuing care was provided in hospital wards, managed by the trust. In site M, it was provided in a building purchased by the health authority, registered as a nursing home, and managed and staffed by a housing association. Some of the places were funded by social services, classified as nursing home beds, but others were funded by the trust, and classified as continuing care beds. The trust was gradually taking over the funding of the nursing home places for someone needing continuing care as each one became vacant. The consultant and staff visited regularly and were very involved with the home. Some joint training was provided for staff, including training in DCM. The quality of the environment was good and the staff appeared to be highly skilled and committed to providing sensitive, individualised care. The cost was £510 per week – considerably less than the cost of a hospital bed.

150. A contrasting arrangement was found in site F, where a nursing home was managed by a housing association in a building leased from the health authority. Individual placements were financed by a combination of social services funding, topped up by the health authority under Section 28a. Although this provision was not strictly considered to be NHS continuing care, and people with very severe behavioural problems could not be accommodated, the top-up funding involved a continuing commitment by the NHS. The total cost was high, at £1,036 per week. Section 28a payments were used in a number of other areas to top up the funding for specialist nursing homes.

151. In some areas, the consultants and health authority have agreed that NHS long-term care in special units should not be expected to continue for life, but only for a period of months or possibly years, while someone's behaviour remains challenging. Individuals could move to a less intensively supported setting when their needs change. The Royal Colleges of Psychiatrists and Physicians have suggested that this model can be effective (Ref. 87). Its advantages include making the best use of specialist staff skills in managing challenging behaviour and meeting individual needs. But there are difficulties too, as vulnerable older people have to make additional moves – which is known to be detrimental, leading to depression, worsening confusion and increasing mortality. In addition, relatives may have been promised care for life, for which they would not have to pay.

152. NHS bodies should not relinquish responsibility for continuing care, but could consider limited moves between units they manage, for a small number of people whose needs change over time. It may be best to provide flexible care in a group of units that are located on a single site. The use of mixed funding, encouraged by the Health Act 1999, may be helpful in this area. It may also be possible for staff to move, rather than residents. For example, NHS staff could provide input to nursing homes on a flexible basis, depending on the current needs. Health and social services should aim to achieve consensus on the criteria for eligibility for continuing NHS care.

RECOMMENDATIONS

4   Hospital and Residential Provision

Providing appropriate hospital treatment, when needed

1   Where the dependency of people with dementia on acute psychiatric wards is low, commissioners and local professionals should review their practices to see whether some could be more appropriately cared for in community settings.

2   Ideally, some mental health beds should be based on the same site as a general hospital, but if staff visit each other and communicate frequently, the difficulties of being physically separate can be overcome. Specialists in mental health and physical care for older people should ensure that they communicate with each other and provide support when it is needed. Effective communication is more important than the organisational structures, and changes to these should be minimised.

3   Providers should aim to make separate living spaces available on wards for those with dementia and those with functional mental illnesses. An appropriate physical environment for wards includes sufficient space for people to walk around safely, a high proportion of single rooms, facilities for those with physical or sensory disabilities, somewhere quiet for relatives to meet with users, privacy for bathing and the availability of stimulating activities and facilities such as chiropody, dental care and hairdressing.

4   Patients who are admitted compulsorily should be visited periodically by the hospital managers or an independent advocate if no one from outside the hospital is taking a continuing interest in their care, as a matter of good practice.

Providing good quality care in residential and nursing homes

5   Commissioners of residential and nursing home care should ensure that sufficient places are available to enable people to leave hospital when they are ready, but not so many that funds are diverted away from services to support people at home.

6   Health and social services should share information and plan together for long-term care, to enable people to be cared for in the most appropriate setting. Pooled budgets that enable a more flexible use of health and social care resources can help to achieve this.

7   Social services should aim to involve a range of professionals, as well as users and carers, in decisions to admit people to residential or nursing home care, to ensure that the services provided best meet the needs of the user.

RECOMMENDATIONS

4 Hospital and Residential Provision

8 Old age psychiatrists and community teams should provide support, advice and guidance to residential and nursing homes that care for large numbers of people with mental health problems. This may help to avoid some hospital admissions and improve the quality of life for residents. It is especially important where individuals in their care have been placed in such homes.

9 Commissioners of health and social care should monitor the number of moves from residential and nursing homes to other residential settings and use this as one indicator of the quality of care provided.

10 Social services should monitor the quality of the care provided in residential and nursing homes, including surveying the views of users and/or carers. They should consider paying higher rates for higher quality provision.

11 Information on the level of dependency, such as CAPE scores, should be used in strategic decision-making about the levels of residential and nursing home provision in the area, to ensure that care is provided for people in the most appropriate setting.

12 Social services should encourage providers in their area to develop some specialist residential care for older people with dementia, and should be prepared to fund places at a higher rate to reflect the specialist skills needed. Some dementia training will be needed in all residential homes, though, as they are all likely to care for some people with dementia.

13 Reviews of each individual's care should continue for at least three to six months, to find out how the placement is working out and to provide support, advice and guidance to the staff. This is particularly important where someone is placed in a setting that is not specialised for mental health.

14 Only a minority of residents of residential and nursing homes with dementia should receive antipsychotic medication, at the lowest possible effective dose, following a careful assessment. The effects should be closely monitored for benefits and adverse effects. Anxiolytics, such as Diazepam, should also be used very sparingly. Medication for all residents of nursing and residential homes should be reviewed regularly.

15 Residents should be assessed to see whether they are suffering from depression, and treated appropriately.

RECOMMENDATIONS

4 Hospital and Residential Provision

17 An appropriate physical environment should include having space for people to walk around safely, colour-coded doors to help people to identify rooms, single bedrooms that people can use when they wish, facilities for those with physical or sensory disabilities, somewhere quiet for relatives to meet with residents, privacy for bathing, and the availability of facilities such as chiropody, dental care and hairdressing. The decoration should be homely and welcoming. Space for therapeutic and other activities, and a garden, are also important. Ideally, residents should live in groups of 12 or less – ideally as few as eight living together. Residents should be encouraged to bring their own furnishings and belongings. Providing a variety of appropriate and stimulating activities is also important.

Providing NHS continuing care when needed

18 NHS bodies should not relinquish responsibility for continuing care, but should consider limited moves between units they manage, for a small number of people whose needs change over time. The use of mixed funding, such as Section 28a, may be helpful in this area. It may also be possible for staff to move, rather than residents. For example, NHS staff could provide input to nursing homes on a flexible basis, depending on the current needs. Health and social services should aim to achieve consensus on the criteria for eligibility for continuing NHS care.

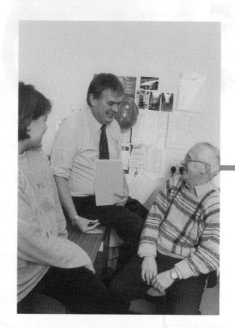

5

Co-ordination between Services

Multidisciplinary community mental health teams can be the centre of a good community service, enabling users to gain access to a wide range of services. Health and social services need to share information with each other and to co-ordinate with GPs, voluntary organisations and general health services for older people.

Community mental health teams (CMHTs)

153. Good co-ordination between health and social services agencies can greatly enhance the quality and effectiveness of services for older people with mental health problems. Community-based professionals need to have ready access to a range of flexible services, including the practical and therapeutic resources of both agencies, in order to help users and carers appropriately.

154. Multidisciplinary CMHTs are the most commonly used approach to joint working between agencies, although the composition of the teams varies. In order to be considered a CMHT, a team needs to have at least two professions working together, meeting at least once a week to discuss referrals and current cases. Consultant psychiatrists described themselves as members of multidisciplinary teams in 6 of the 12 sites [EXHIBIT 32]. They would share some cases with colleagues, attend the weekly meeting and make themselves available to team members at other times. Other consultants considered themselves to be team leaders, who decided what the members did and used them as resources to help out in some elements of care and treatment. GPs in sites where consultants described themselves as members of CMHTs more often agreed with the statement

EXHIBIT 32

Membership of CMHTs (community mental health teams)

Consultant psychiatrists described themselves as members of multidisciplinary teams in six sites.

Multidisciplinary CMHTs available. Including:	STUDY SITES											
	A	B	C	D	E	F	G	H	J	K	L	M
Consultants	X	N/A	X	X	X	✓	✓	✓	X	✓	✓	✓
CPNs	✓	N/A	✓	✓	✓	✓	✓	✓	✓	✓	✓	✓
Social workers	X	N/A	✓	X	✓	✓	X	✓	X	✓	X	✓
Psychologists	X	N/A	X	X	✓	✓	X	✓	X	✓	X	X
Occupational therapists	X	N/A	X	X	✓	✓	✓	✓	✓	✓	X	X
Physiotherapists	X	N/A	X	X	✓	X	✓	X	✓	✓	X	X

Source: Audit Commission checklist

'I have ready access, when required, to specialist advice to help me diagnose and manage dementia' than those in other areas.[I] In addition, they agreed more often with the statement that 'There are satisfactory specialised services… in my area to meet the needs of those with dementia'.[II] They were also more likely to agree with equivalent statements in relation to depression, but the association was weaker.

155. CPNs were employed in all 12 study sites, social workers were members of the teams in 6 sites, OTs in 6, physiotherapists in 4 and psychologists in 4. All of these professions have important contributions to make. Team members should also make links with other services such as social work, day care and hospital wards. GPs and primary care teams need to be kept informed about the work of the teams and new service developments. Links with other services such as chiropody and the community dental service are also important, as many users of the mental health services will also need to use them.

Team management

156. The management of multidisciplinary teams needs careful planning, especially where different agencies are involved. Decisions need to be made about the roles of the different professionals, stating which tasks can be carried out by all members and which require the unique skills of a particular profession. The manager in one local authority had recently withdrawn the social workers from a multi-agency team because he felt that their expertise was not being used effectively. All team members had appeared to be working as 'junior doctors' under the management of the consultant. The manager's concerns were not unfounded, as the case files of a number of users were found to contain letters from a social worker, advising the GP about changes in medication.

157. The extent of joint working in multidisciplinary teams varied. In site E the team members shared an office base but made formal referrals, on paper, to their colleagues in other disciplines. Each group kept a separate set of files. This arrangement led to occasional delays and sometimes created unnecessary paperwork. In site J, there were no specialist social work posts for mental health for older people and no social workers in the CMHTs. However, two small projects funded by MISG provided one-half of a social work post in a CPN base and one-half of a CPN post in a social work base. Although these projects were successful, they had been unable to bring the resources of the mainstream agencies closer together.

I   Significant at .005 level, using Student's t-Test.

II   Significant at .05 level, using Student's t-Test.

The teams that were most successful at communicating contained a mix of professions, working from the same office

158. In four sites the collaborative arrangements appeared to be working well. In site L, a social services building provided the base for a resource centre, with residential beds, respite care, day care and the CMHT, although social workers were not members of CMHTs. Having a common location meant that health professionals, care managers and resource centre staff were in frequent contact and developed trust and mutual respect. This helped them to access each other's resources easily.

159. In site H, the agencies were in the process of establishing a joint mental health trust, in which health and social services resources were to be pooled. The social workers attended all team meetings, but they could not take referrals directly from CPNs. Access to day care could be agreed within the team, but decisions on residential and nursing home care needed approval by a team manager, with input from a CPN. A small jointly staffed resource centre had been developed.

160. In site K, any member of the multidisciplinary team could arrange for home care, day care, residential or nursing home care, which meant that services could be put in place rapidly. Decisions involving a budget over a given level had to be approved by the local social services manager. Some of the home care organisers attended the CMHT meetings. The OTs in the team provided training for home care-workers who worked with people with mental health problems.

161. The teams that were most successful at communicating contained a mix of professions, working from the same office, as in Bridgend **[CASE STUDY 12]**. Some tasks could be carried out by any profession but others used the specific skills of a particular discipline. The teams that appeared to be most effective in providing flexible and responsive help for users and carers had resources readily available so that practical or therapeutic help could be given without delay. Joint training proved to be an effective way to promote joint work as well as to develop appropriate skills.

162. Health and social services agencies should develop arrangements to facilitate the exchange of information and the sharing of expertise over individual cases. While maintaining confidentiality for users is essential, this should not inhibit the effective exchange of information within teams. Those planning the service should ensure that the resources of each agency can be accessed easily and quickly by all specialist professionals, without involving over-bureaucratic procedures (for example, requests for multiple reports). The best way to achieve this is usually through a CMHT, in which consultants are also members. If a GP specifically requests an assessment by a consultant this should be provided. In other cases, a first home visit can be carried out by either a psychiatrist or another member of the CMHT, depending on the person's needs and local service arrangements.

CASE STUDY 12

The Bridgend community care teams

- Four very small locality teams of CPNs and social workers share offices and discuss individual cases informally.

- Each profession can request resources from both agencies.

- Three teams have a devolved budget in the form of specialist home-care hours, to use at their discretion, to provide flexible care.

- The consultant gives advice on a flexible basis and attends regular team meetings.

- Respite care is available from both health and social services, and can be allocated by agreement between team members.

- Initial funding came through a special grant and subsequent support is ring-fenced within social services.

- Other local resources included a 'Care and Repair' scheme, funded through a local authority grant [CASE STUDY 6, p48].

Shared assessment and care management

163. The effective assessment and management of an individual's care is essential. Many older people, especially those with dementia, have complex needs for both health and social care. For these people, assessments in which different professionals see the user together on at least one occasion can lead to a better shared understanding of the situation, provided that they are managed sensitively. They can avoid the user having to provide the same information several times, and help them to feel that their care is consistent and co-ordinated. The use of joint assessments is an indicator of collaborative working, and demonstrates that needs are being assessed in a comprehensive way, although they may not be necessary for everyone.

164. The number of assessments that are carried out jointly, by more than one profession or agency (as recorded in case files), varies from almost none to almost all cases [EXHIBIT 33, overleaf]. In four sites, over one-half of the users whose files were examined had received at least one joint multidisciplinary assessment, but only in two sites had more than one-half of the users received a joint multi-agency assessment. One of these was site H, where a joint health and social services trust was being set up. CMHTs should have clear policies and protocols for assessment, including the use of multidisciplinary and multi-agency assessments. Users with complex needs should receive at least one multidisciplinary assessment at an early stage after referral to the service and joint reviews at intervals afterwards. Any risk the individual may present to themselves or others should be included in the assessment.

EXHIBIT 33

The use of joint multidisciplinary and multi-agency assessments

In only two sites had more than one-half of the users received a joint multi-agency assessment.

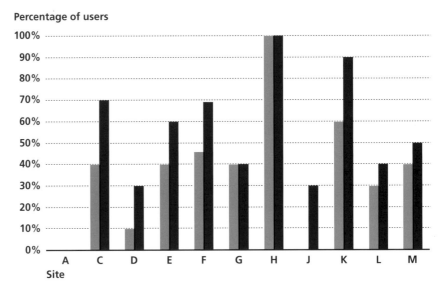

Percentage of users

■ At least one multi-agency assessment

■ At least one multidisciplinary assessment

Note: 'Assessments' here include reviews.

Source: Audit Commission survey of case files

165. The assessment process should result in a clear understanding of the needs of the individual and a plan for addressing them, in which the user or a representative has been involved. It should reflect the contributions of all relevant agencies and copies of individual care plans should be given to users. The plan needs to be co-ordinated by a key worker who is in touch with all of the relevant agencies and services. In England, the Care Programme Approach (CPA) provides a standardised approach to assessment and care planning. Originally devised for younger adults, it can appropriately be used for older people and identifies three levels of need. Level one is generally for users whose needs can be met through a single agency. Level two is for those who need contributions from two or more agencies and level three for users with highly complex needs.

166. In Wales, thorough assessment and care planning are needed in a similar way, reflecting different levels of need, but the CPA is not formally required. However, the CPA was being used in one of the sites in Wales. Ideally, the minimum documentation to fulfil all the requirements should be used, including a single care plan and case files.

167. Although community professionals reported that 70 per cent of the users on their caseloads had care programmes, few of the files contained CPA documentation [EXHIBIT 34]. In sites H and K, there were CPA forms in all of the case files, but in other sites less than one-half of the case files included these forms. In six sites, users in the community had key workers. GPs in these six sites were more likely to agree with the statements 'I have ready access to specialist advice to help me diagnose and manage dementia'[I] and 'there are satisfactory specialised services for older people and their families in my area to meet the needs of those with dementia',[II] than in other areas.

168. Local service managers should either use the CPA or make sure that its aims are achieved in some other way. The use of structured, comprehensive need assessments should be encouraged (Ref. 88). The CPA needs to dovetail with local arrangements for care management in social services. If not, there is a danger that multiple assessments are still required, reducing the benefit of joint assessment and team working. In England, if CPA is applied, the information should be recorded in case files and should be available to all agencies. In Wales, equivalent information about the contributions of relevant agencies should be recorded.

I   Significant at the .005 level, using Student's t-Test.

II   Significant at the .01 level, using Student's t-Test.

EXHIBIT 34

CPA documentation in case files

Few case files contained CPA documentation.

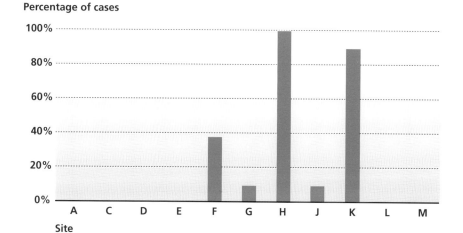

Percentage of cases

Source: Audit Commission survey of case files

Flexible access to services

169. If users' needs are to be met effectively, as identified in their care programme, their key worker needs to have ready access to a range of different services. This depends on good communication between the agencies and arrangements that facilitate access. The number of services received by users is an indicator of joint working. The mean number of services received by users living in the community varied from more than four in site C (where local multidisciplinary teams worked closely with other service providers) to only two in some of the sites that had less developed joint working [EXHIBIT 35]. The services included:

- home care;
- meals on wheels;
- sitting and befriending services;
- district nurse;
- CPN;
- social worker;
- outpatients department;
- day hospital;
- day centre;
- respite care in a residential or nursing home; and
- respite care in hospital.

170. The extent to which users whose key worker is a CPN also receive care from social services is another indicator of co-ordination between the agencies. In two sites more than 50 per cent of those with a CPN key-worker were receiving social services home care, but in one, fewer than 10 per cent did [EXHIBIT 36]. The two sites with the highest score on this indicator had specialist home-care workers for mental health. The provision of specialist workers can help to promote co-ordination between health and social services since fewer individuals with greater expertise are involved.

171. Sharing information is essential if needs are to be met effectively. If information about care provided by one agency is absent from the other agency's files, the key-worker will have an incomplete picture of the user's situation and needs. He or she might also miss out on useful professional contacts when decisions are made about their care, and services are likely to be used inefficiently. So the information in case files needs to be comprehensive.

EXHIBIT 35

The mean number of services received by users in the community

The mean number of services received varied from more than four where local multidisciplinary teams worked together closely, to only two in sites with less developed joint working.

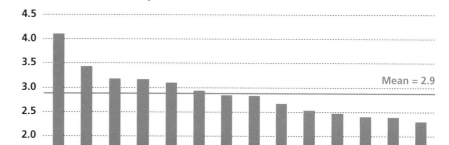

Mean number of services per user

Mean = 2.9

Site

Source: Audit Commission survey of individual case information

EXHIBIT 36

Percentage of users with CPN key-workers who were receiving home care through social services

In two sites more than 50 per cent of those with a CPN key-worker were receiving social services home care, but in one, fewer than 10 per cent did.

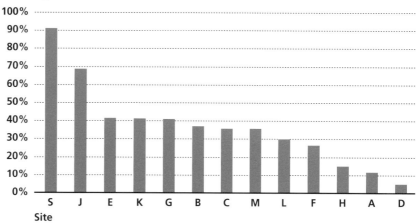

Percentage of users

Site

Source: Audit Commission survey of individual case information

172. The information about social care held in 'health' case files varies, however. In one site, all the health files (used by CPNs and other health professionals) examined contained details of the social care received by users, but in others only around one-third did [EXHIBIT 37]. Site H, in which social care information was present in all files, was in the process of setting up a joint health and social care trust. In some of the other sites, users may have been receiving social care but the details were not present in the files. In site C, where 90 per cent of cases had social care details in the health files, the health and social services case files were joined together and both agencies had equal access to them. None of the sites had fully shared case files. Nor had shared information systems been developed in any of the sites. Shared case files between health and social services are the ideal but, if this is not possible, each agency's files should contain details of the services provided through the other agency, as part of a shared plan.

EXHIBIT 37

The inclusion of social care information in health case files

In one site all the health files contained details of social care but in others only around one-third did.

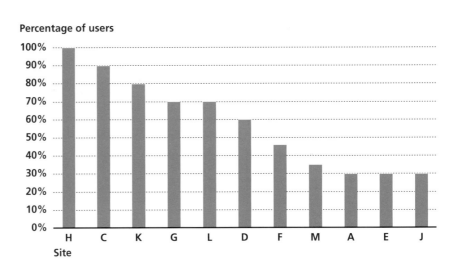

Percentage of users

Source: Audit Commission survey of case files

Co-ordination with other services

173. Voluntary organisations often play a major role in mental health services for older people. Sometimes they provide additional services to the statutory providers, such as advocacy and information (as in Case Studies 2 and 3). In some areas, they provide mainstream services such as day care, funded by health or social services. In others, they have a significant role in planning and delivering local services in conjunction with the statutory agencies. The Petersfield Centre has developed in this way with Age Concern as one of the initiators and main participants [CASE STUDY 13].

CASE STUDY 13

The Petersfield Centre, Havering

The centre houses a day unit, a memory clinic, a CPN team, the Age Concern support service, and an office base for social services staff, including specialist home carers for older people with mental health needs. The reception area is run by Age Concern, which some users and carers find easier to accept than statutory services. The services are solely for those with dementia. There is another team of CPNs who work with older people with functional mental health problems.

The day unit provides 15 places and is available on a long-term basis, usually until people have to move into residential or nursing home care. The memory clinic has a multidisciplinary team with a psychologist, a psychiatrist, a nurse and a speech and language therapist. Team members visit people at home as well as seeing them in the clinic. At least three visits are made and informed consent given before antidementia drugs are prescribed. Age Concern provides advice and support, by telephone and through home visits; carer support groups; written information and a library; and advocacy by trained volunteers. The health authority pays the rent for the building.

Most people contact the Age Concern service directly, although some are referred by their GP, CPN or social worker. It is evaluated through regular meetings with carers' forums to find out what aspects of the service are most important. In addition, evaluation questionnaires are sent to all carers who have used it.

The project began in 1993, with the aim of improving services to carers. The joint planning group of Barking and Havering Health Authority, Barking, Havering and Brentwood Community Trust and Havering Social Services created a task group, including voluntary organisations and carers' representatives. Some funding became available from the closure of the local psychiatric hospital. The involvement of the health authority was instrumental, especially in the early stages.

Communication and support needs to go both ways, as many older people have both physical and mental health problems

174. The importance of links with GP practices was highlighted in Chapter 2. GPs and primary care teams can benefit from contact with the specialist services, especially when there is a named worker that they can get to know. Consultants and other members of CMHTs should be able to provide advice and support to primary care teams in diagnosing and managing the care of older people with mental health problems. GPs' ratings of the local support and advice available were higher in areas with linked workers from social services (see Chapter 2).

175. The need for specialist mental health professionals to provide support to residential and nursing homes was outlined in Chapter 4. This can help to avoid some admissions to hospital or transfers to other nursing homes and can also help staff to provide a better environment for those in their care.

176. The importance of liaison with geriatric medicine and other services responsible for the physical health care of older people was also noted in Chapter 4. For example, those in the care of mental health services or in residential or nursing homes may suffer pain but be unable to express it, except through problematic behaviour. Communication and support needs to go both ways, as many older people have both physical and mental health problems. Although the links between services are crucial, it is more important to make the existing linkages work well than to introduce organisational changes that can be disruptive for users and carers as well as for staff. Links with mental health services for younger people are also important, especially in relation to younger people with dementia and people with long-standing mental health problems. Joint professional training in matters such as the use of the Mental Health Act can also be useful.

177. Commissioners of mental health services for older people can bring together the perspectives of these different groups and use them in developing a local strategy. The roles of strategic management and commissioning are the subject of the next chapter.

RECOMMENDATIONS

5 Co-ordination between Services

To create a comprehensive and co-ordinated service for users and their carers

1   Health and social services agencies should develop arrangements to facilitate the exchange of information and the sharing of expertise over individual cases. They should ensure that the resources of each agency can be accessed easily and quickly by all specialist professionals, without involving over-bureaucratic procedures (for example, requests for multiple reports). The best way to achieve this is usually through a CMHT, in which consultants are also members.

2   Older people with complex needs for both health and social care should receive at least one joint assessment at an early stage after referral to the service and occasional joint reviews at intervals afterwards.

3   Local service managers should either use the Care Programme Approach (CPA) or make sure that its aims are achieved in some other way. It needs to dovetail with local arrangements for care management in social services. If not, there is a danger that multiple assessments are still required, reducing the benefit of joint assessment and team working. In England, CPA information should be recorded in case files and should be available to all agencies. In Wales, equivalent information about the contributions of relevant agencies should be recorded.

4   The provision of specialist home care-workers can help to promote co-ordination between health and social services.

5   Shared case files between health and social services are the ideal but, if this is not possible, each agency's files should contain details of the services provided through the other agency, as part of a shared plan.

6

Developing a Comprehensive Strategy

Commissioners have a key role in drawing together all the elements of a comprehensive service and in setting priorities and targets.

Developing a shared vision

178. The evidence in the previous chapters shows that services for older people with mental health problems are patchy and inconsistent across the country, and often fail to link together into a coherent service network. All of the elements of a comprehensive mental health service for older people, described in the preceding chapters, need to be drawn together at the strategic level. The goals of the service should include the intended balance between home-based, day, outpatient and hospital services, as well as the mix of long-term care provided by residential homes, nursing homes and NHS-funded continuing care beds. A complete strategy should include a policy on the involvement of users and carers in assessments and decisions about their care.

179. Commissioners have a key role in setting priorities and targets for the service, but health commissioners in only 4 of the 12 areas visited had definite goals and plans for the future shape of the service. In most of the other areas the service was shaped by providers who generally had clearer views than commissioners about what should be provided and how it should be organised. Consultant psychiatrists usually had the greatest influence on the way services developed, except in two sites (H and K). In these areas, plans had been set out by a group of managers and professionals from health and social services. New consultants had been recruited who were willing to adapt their working practices to the joint plans. In one of these (site H) the health commissioners played an active part.

180. Local strategies should include both health and local authority services, and should work towards joint commissioning, as emphasised by national policy. In England, the 'Better Services for Vulnerable People' initiative requires annual Joint Investment Plans (JIPs) to be drawn up, with details of the resources of both agencies, and the outcomes that they intend to achieve together. The JIP, in turn, is one element of the Health Improvement Programme. A survey of the first round of JIPs indicated that information on current expenditure and activity was often patchy and confused, although the stronger plans had provided an analysis of service gaps and priorities (Ref. 89). Most of the plans for mental health care for older people were underdeveloped, so special attention needs to be focused on this group. Only one-quarter of the plans indicated active involvement with PCGs. The audits that follow this report should help local agencies in England and Wales to learn more about the activity, costs and performance of services within JIP areas, and so work towards improving care for older people with mental health problems.

The number of people with moderate or severe dementia in the local population can be estimated from a model based on age profiles

181. The *Partnership in Action* document in England, and *Partnership for Improvement* in Wales (Refs. 7 and 8), aim to facilitate the joint commissioning of services. The NHS Act 1999 (Ref. 9), which enables more flexible financial transfers between agencies and the development of new joint agencies, should assist commissioners in developing appropriate arrangements to suit local circumstances. To help this process, attention needs to be paid nationally to addressing the different terms and conditions of employment of health and social services staff. Voluntary organisations and support groups for users and carers can also make important contributions to the planning of services. It is essential that the different groups involved have a shared vision concerning priorities and the way forward. In some areas, the commissioning and provision arrangements are undergoing major change, with the development of PCGs or trusts in England and local health groups in Wales. Where this is the case, it is especially important that the service remains based on these principles and that joint working across agencies is strengthened rather than disrupted.

182. Commissioners in health and local authorities should take the lead in setting out strategic goals and priorities, in conjunction with users and carers, professionals, service managers and other groups such as independent service providers. While jointly commissioned services with shared budgets may be the ideal, they should aim for a co-ordinated service, while minimising organisational change as far as possible. Where there is no shared vision, one of the authorities will need to take a lead in championing a policy that takes this forward.

Estimating need

183. Demographic information can help planners to gauge the needs of their local population for mental health care. Age is the main factor influencing the prevalence of dementia, but functional mental health problems may vary with social factors such as isolation and low income. The number of people with moderate or severe dementia in the local population can be estimated from a model based on age profiles that has been validated by disability surveys of the Office of Population Censuses and Surveys (OPCS) (Ref. 25). Local planners can obtain an estimate for their population by entering the numbers in the broad age bands 65–74, 75–84 and 85 and over. The model provides estimates of the total numbers of people with dementia with problems with self-care, mobility, incontinence and aggressive behaviour. It also estimates the numbers of such people who are living in the community, alone or with others, and the numbers with high needs or 'critical interval needs' for care (defined as needing care or supervision continually or at brief irregular intervals each day). This gives an indication of the level of local need.

184. Needs vary, as indicated by the number of people with dementia with 'critical interval' needs per 10,000 population over 65. The model only takes account of people with dementia, not those with functional mental health problems such as depression, but it provides a starting point. Expenditure on specialist mental health services also varies, but not in relation to need [EXHIBIT 38]. Planners and commissioners should use the comparative information provided by this model to inform their planning for local services. The actual numbers produced will not correspond to the likely number of service users, as only a percentage will require help from specialist professionals. However, the figures can provide a basis for comparisons with the level of resources provided elsewhere for a similar population.

185. Planners and commissioners should use estimates of the numbers of people likely to experience mental health problems from demographic data, compared with other areas, to inform their planning of the level of resources needed.

EXHIBIT 38

The number of people with dementia in the community with 'critical interval need' for care and the expenditure on specialist services per 10,000 population over 65

Expenditure on specialist mental health services varies, but not in relation to need.

Expenditure (£000)

Number in need of critical interval care per 10,000 population over 65

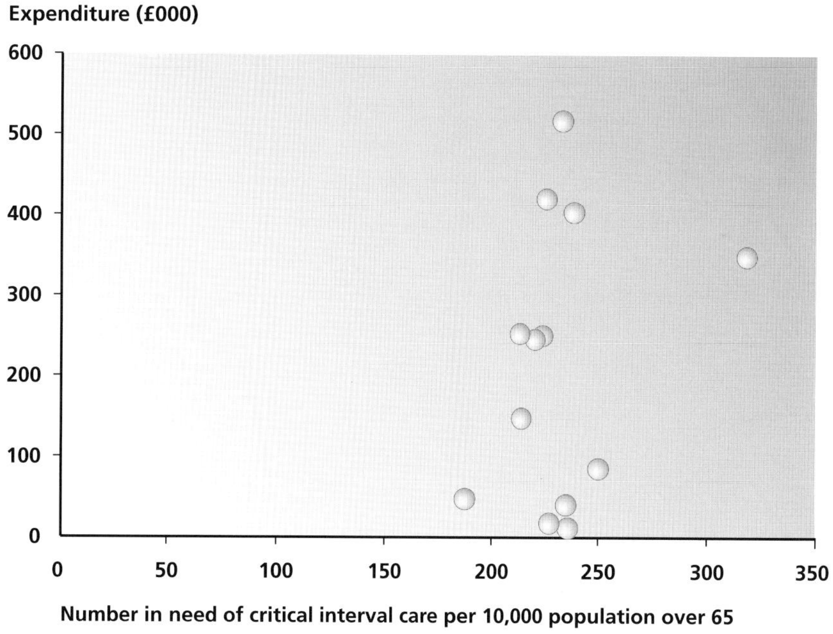

Source: Cambridge cognitive disability planning model; Audit Commission resource mapping survey

Reviewing current provision

186. Obtaining good quality information about current services is the starting point from which future plans can be developed. A national survey in 1997 found the level of information about local needs and service provision for people with dementia to be very patchy. Only one health authority in five was able to identify its expenditure in this area (Ref. 90). Identifying expenditure on older people with functional mental health problems was even more difficult in most of the study sites. In only two sites did someone in the health authority have a specific responsibility for gathering information about local services. This had been prompted by the need for detailed information to complete the JIPs required by the Department of Health under the Better Services for Vulnerable People initiative.

187. As part of this study, data about the level of service provision (number of staff, places, expenditure, and activity) by health authorities, trusts and local authorities were collected for JIP areas across England and local health group areas in Wales. This was the first phase of the audit of mental health services for older people. Information on current expenditure and activity in mental health services for older people should be produced on a regular basis to facilitate planning and to inform budget allocations. Knowledge about existing services can form the basis for specific targets to be achieved in future years.

Monitoring delivery

188. More detailed information about the quality of service provision can help to inform strategic planners and commissioners about what is working well. For example, the CAPE scores of people in various settings indicate how far the services manage to support highly dependent people at home. Other useful indicators include carers' views of local services, GPs' views of local services, and unmet needs in selected groups of users. This kind of information should help health and social care agencies to recognise each other's strengths and capabilities, and is to be collected by auditors during the forthcoming audits. Those commissioning services should use monitoring information on service quality to inform their plans.

189. In this study GPs rated the level of specialist support and advice for diagnosing and managing mental health problems in older people more highly in areas with:

- consultants who were members of CMHTs;
- key workers in community teams;
- CPA in operation;
- a memory clinic;
- the availability of antidementia drugs; and
- positive efforts to contact and educate GPs [TABLE 2].[1]

---

1   See previous chapters for details of statistical tests.

190. The level of GP satisfaction with services was found to be higher in areas with:

- CPA;
- a memory clinic;
- the availability of antidementia drugs; and
- positive efforts to contact and educate GPs [TABLE 2].[1]

191. The most frequent comment from GPs was that specialist services were understaffed, underfunded or lacked support, but many others said the services were good or satisfactory. Some GPs in site L described the specialist advice available as 'excellent' but those in sites A and D said that specialist services were slow to respond to requests for help. GPs in sites D, J and L said that there was a shortage of specialist support services for older people with mental health needs, especially support for families and carers; day provision, including social activities; and respite care. A need for more day hospitals, more CPNs and more social services back-up was also mentioned by some GPs. In site K the local ADS sitting and befriending service was highly praised by both GPs and carers.

---

[1]   See previous chapters for details of statistical tests.

TABLE 2

Associations between GP satisfaction and features of specialist services

| Statement | Percentage of GPs who agree that there are satisfactory services locally for: | | | |
| | Dementia | | Depression | |
Service feature	present	absent	present	absent
Consultants in CMHTs	52.4	47.8	52.1	48.3
Key-worker in CMHTs	52.3	47.9	52.1	48.5
CPA	55.9	45.8	54.7	47
Memory clinic	53.6	45.6	52.8	47
Antidementia drugs available	54.5	42.5	53.3	45.2
NHS continuing care	49.5	51.9	51.1	49.9
Special efforts to educate GPs	55.9	46.5	54.5	47.6

192. The most frequent comments from carers of people with dementia were that more respite care was needed, followed by more help at home and more day care. Several also said that they would like more information about the illness and more social contact. Only one-third of carers said that they had been told about how to care for their relative safely and to cope with dementia, and just over one-half said that a doctor or nurse regularly reviews their relative's condition.

193. 'Process' measures are also useful, such as the referral sources for different services, the length of stay, the use of CPA, the use of home-based assessments, the use of joint multi-agency and multidisciplinary assessments, and the involvement of users and/or carers in decisions. Reviewing the pathways of some individuals through services could also provide useful information about how well services are working together.

194. A sample of case files was examined in each site to see whether the views of users or carers contributed to assessments and reviews. The percentage of cases in which their views were explicitly recorded or taken into account varied. Only around 10 per cent of the files contained documents that had been signed by either the user or carer [EXHIBIT 39]. In only one site were copies of assessments, care plans and reviews routinely given to users or carers. A comprehensive strategy should include a policy on the involvement of users and carers in assessments and decisions about their care. Case records should include information about the involvement of users and carers in decision-making, as well as copies of any documents signed by them. Copies should be given to the users and/or carers.

Identifying gaps in services

195. Planners also need to monitor services to identify where there are shortfalls or gaps. In this study the unmet needs of users were identified by staff who knew the users well. The unmet needs noted most frequently included regular, appropriate day-time activities and regular social contact [EXHIBIT 40]. [1]

---

1   Based on a list from the Camberwell Assessment of Need for the Elderly (Ref. 88).

User and carer involvement in assessments and reviews

Only about 10 per cent of the files contained documents that had been signed by either the user or carer.

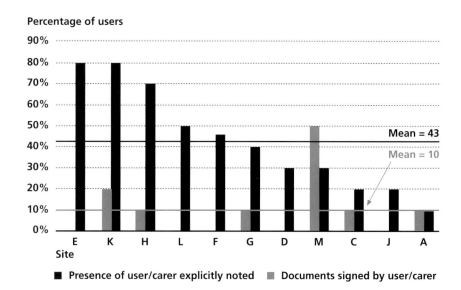

Percentage of users

Mean = 43

Mean = 10

Site

■ Presence of user/carer explicitly noted   ■ Documents signed by user/carer

Source: Audit Commission survey of case files

The unmet needs of users (defined by staff)

The unmet needs noted most frequently included regular, appropriate day-time activities and regular social contact.

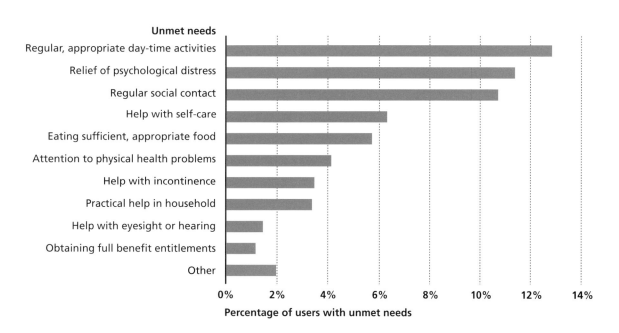

Unmet needs

Regular, appropriate day-time activities
Relief of psychological distress
Regular social contact
Help with self-care
Eating sufficient, appropriate food
Attention to physical health problems
Help with incontinence
Practical help in household
Help with eyesight or hearing
Obtaining full benefit entitlements
Other

Percentage of users with unmet needs

Source: Audit Commission survey of individual case information

Developing services

Health and social services

196. Mental health services for older people need to be planned jointly by health and social services, to make the best use of the resources available. They were planned in this way in 5 of the 12 sites (C, H, K, L, M), with each agency's plans jointly owned and taking account of each other's resources. Some joint services had been developed, including CMHTs with shared premises and resources from both sides. In three sites, joint resource centres had been developed, combining day provision with respite and residential care and staffed by health and social services staff, working together. In some cases the building was owned by social services, in others by health. One example of this is the Ridley Day Service in Somerset [CASE STUDY 14].

197. The responsibility for supporting older people with mental health problems should be shared by both health and social services. Some of the short-term assessment and treatment may best be provided by health agencies and some social care by social services, but much can be shared. Long-term responsibilities can fall to either agency, so planning in this area needs to be jointly carried out so as to make best use of limited resources. Commissioners of services should take the lead in this area, and should consider whether jointly managed services may be appropriate in their area. Planning for generic provision also needs to take account of people with mental health problems who are likely to use the services.

CASE STUDY 14

The Ridley Day Service, Somerset

This provides 20 health and social care day places on 6 days of the week, 2 days for people with functional problems, 2 for those with dementia and 2 'mixed' days. The staff also visit people at home. The building is on a hospital site. It was provided by the Health Authority and it is staffed jointly by nursing and social work staff, with the assistance of a number of volunteers. There is a weekly meeting which the consultant attends. The unit is linked with provision for respite care, both in a six-bedded unit in the hospital on the same site and in a residential home nearby.

The unit developed from a close working relationship between the NHS trust and social services. Since the unit was set up, a jointly commissioned, integrated health and social care trust with a jointly managed budget has been formed.

Mental health services for older people need to be planned jointly by health and social services, to make the best use of the resources available

Involving other groups

198. Voluntary organisations and support groups for users and carers can make important contributions to the planning of services. The Petersfield Centre was largely shaped by the combined efforts of statutory and voluntary groups (Case Study 13, Chapter 5).

Service agreements

199. Commissioning services can provide an opportunity to raise quality standards and to keep regular checks on what services are doing. Service agreements with providers should include a requirement to provide regular information on the levels of service provision and activities, as well as information on quality. Quality indicators could include the physical environment, the training and support arrangements for staff and the use of processes such as dementia care mapping in residential settings. Developing standards for an additional 'quality premium' (see para. 137, Chapter 4) could improve the quality of services. The standards could be assessed by commissioners, providers and independent groups such as local carers' organisations.

Learning and innovation

200. Commissioners and provider managers should play a part in stimulating innovation and good practice, by circulating information about best practice and promoting discussion and debate. This should be backed with research evidence where possible. It also needs to be complemented by an approach that encourages new initiatives and pilots new approaches, which can be monitored and lessons learned about what works and what is less successful. In this way, commissioners, providers and users and carers can all contribute to improving the quality of care for older people with mental health problems – promoting care at home where possible, releasing resources from expensive hospital and nursing home care.

RECOMMENDATIONS

6 Developing a Comprehensive Strategy

To ensure that the vision for the future direction of mental health services is shared by all those involved

1 Commissioners in health and local authorities should take the lead in setting out strategic goals and priorities, in conjunction with users and carers, professionals, service managers and other groups such as independent service providers. While jointly commissioned services with shared budgets may be the ideal, they should aim for a co-ordinated service, while minimising organisational change as far as possible.

To ensure that provision is appropriate to local needs and circumstances

2 Planners and commissioners should use estimates from demographic data of the numbers of people likely to experience mental health problems, compared with other areas, to inform their planning of the level of resources needed.

3 Information about current service provision (number of staff, places, expenditure and activity) should be produced on a regular basis to facilitate planning and to inform budget allocations.

To keep a check on the quality of service provision

4 A comprehensive strategy should include a policy on the involvement of users and carers in assessments and decisions about their care. Case records should include information about the involvement of users and carers in decision-making, as well as copies of any documents signed by them. Copies should be given to the users and/or carers.

5 Commissioners of mental health services should make use of process and outcome indicators to assess how well the services are succeeding in their aims. Outcome indicators could include carers' views of local services, GPs' views of local services, unmet needs in selected groups of users, and the participation of users and carers in their care.

6 Service agreements with providers should require regular information about levels of service provision and activities, including information on quality.

RECOMMENDATIONS

6 Developing a Comprehensive Strategy

To make the best use of the resources of all agencies

7   Health and social services should share the responsibility for supporting older people with mental health problems. Commissioners of services should take the lead in this area, and should consider whether jointly managed services may be appropriate in their area. Planning for generic provision also needs to take account of people with mental health problems who are likely to use the services.

8   Commissioners and provider managers should play a part in stimulating innovation and good practice by circulating information about best practice and promoting discussion and debate. This should be backed with research evidence where possible. It also needs to be complemented by an approach that stimulates new initiatives and pilots new approaches. These should be monitored and lessons learned from them about what works and what is less successful.

Appendix 1

Advisory group

Tom Dening	Consultant Psychiatrist, Addenbrooke's NHS Trust, Cambridge and the Department of Health
Peter Dunn	Social Services Inspectorate
Clive Evers	The Alzheimer's Society (formerly The Alzheimer's Disease Society)
Andrew Fairbairn	Consultant Old Age Psychiatrist, Newcastle City Health Trust
Enid Levin	National Institute for Social Work
Jenny Finch	HAS 2000
Gill Herbert and Mary Godfrey	Nuffield Institute for Health
Stephen Iliffe	Department of Primary Care and Population Sciences, Royal Free Hospital, London
Tom Kitwood (late)	Bradford Dementia Centre
Rosalynd Lowe	Audit Commissioner and Chief Executive, Hounslow and Spelthorne Community and Mental Health NHS Trust
Mary Marshall	Director, Dementia Services Development Centre, University of Stirling
Alisoun Milne	Lecturer in the Care of Older People, University of Kent at Canterbury
Martin Orrell	Consultant Psychiatrist and Reader in Ageing and Mental Health, UCL Medical School
Phil Rees	CPN, Bridgend and District NHS Trust
Neil Walker	Shaftesbury Society and Association of Directors of Social Services
Sir Ronald Watson	Audit Commissioner

References

1. Government Actuary's Department, *1994-based Population Projections*, personal communication.

2. L Blom-Cooper, H Hally and E Murphy, *The Falling Shadow*, Duckworth, London, 1995.

3. Department of Health, *A Handbook on the Mental Health of Older People*, HMSO, 1997.

4. Royal Commission on Long Term Care, *With Respect to Old Age: Long Term Care – Rights and Responsibilities*, the Stationery Office, 1999.

5. Royal College of Psychiatrists and Royal College of Physicians, *The Care of Older People with Mental Illness: Specialist Services and Medical Training*, Royal Colleges, 1998.

6. Department of Health, *Better Services for Vulnerable People*, EL (97) 62, CI (97) 24, 1997.

7. Department of Health, *Partnership in Action*, NHS Executive, 1998.

8. Welsh Office, *Partnership for Improvement*, Welsh Office, 1998.

9. Department of Health, *National Health Service Act 1999*.

10. Department of Health, *The Carers' Recognition and Service Act 1995*.

11. J Beech and L Harding, *Assessment of the Elderly*, NFER/Nelson, 1990.

12. J Copeland, M Abou-Saleb and D Blazer, *Principles and Practice of Geriatric Psychiatry*, Wiley, 1994.

13. A Milne, *GP Survey*, Tizard Centre, University of Kent, 1998.

14. M Roth, F Huppert, E Tym and C Mountjoy, *CAMDEX: The Cambridge Examination for Mental Disorders of the Elderly*, Cambridge University Press, 1988.

15. B Isaacs and Y Neville, *The Measurement of Need in Old People*, Scottish Home and Health Department, Edinburgh, 1975.

16. A Henderson, *Dementia*, World Health Organisation, Geneva, 1994.

17. F Lai and R Williams, 'A prospective study of Alzheimer's Disease in Down's Syndrome', *Archives of Neurology*, Vol 46, pp269–87, 1989.

18. W Zigman, N Schupf, M Haveman and M Silverman, *Epidemiology of Alzheimer's Disease in Mental Retardation: Results and Recommendations*, from International conference, Washington, American Association on Mental Retardation, 1995.

19. T Holland, J Hon, F Huppert et al, 'Population based study of the prevalence and presentation of dementia in adults with Down's syndrome', *British Journal of Psychiatry*, Vol. 172, pp493–8, 1998.

20. A Ott, M Breteler et al, 'Prevalence of Alzheimer's Disease and vascular dementia: association with education. The Rotterdam study', *British Medical Journal*, Vol. 310, pp970–3, 1995.

21. A Jorm, A Korten and A Henderson, 'The prevalence of dementia: a quantitative integration of the literature', *Acta Psychiatrica Scandinavica*, Vol. 76, pp465–79, 1987.

22. C Ballard, 'Dementia with Lewy Bodies: An Update', paper presented at 5th World Congress on Innovations in Psychiatry, London, 21 May, 1998.

23. M Orrell and P Bebbington, 'Life events and senile dementia 1: Admission, deterioration and social environment change', *Psychological Medicine*, Vol. 25, pp373–86, 1995.

24. K Anthony, A Proctor, A Silverman et al, 'Mood and behaviour problems following the relocation of elderly patients with a mental illness', *Age and Ageing*, Vol. 16, pp355–65, 1987.

25. M Ely, D Melzer, L Opit and C Brayne, 'Estimating the numbers and characteristics of elderly people with cognitive disability in local populations', *Research, Policy and Planning*, Vol. 14, pp13–18, 1996.

26. Medical Research Council cognitive function and ageing study, 'Cognitive function and dementia in six areas of England and Wales: the distribution of MMSE and prevalence of GMS organicity level in the MRC CFA study', *Psychological Medicine*, Vol. 28, pp319–35, 1998.

27. D Melzer, M Ely and C Brayne, 'Cognitive impairment in elderly people: population based estimate of the future in England, Scotland and Wales', *British Medical Journal*, Vol. 315, p462, 1997.

28. A Mann, N Graham and D Ashby, 'Psychiatric illness in residential homes for the elderly: a survey in one London borough', *Age and Ageing*, Vol. 13, pp257–65, 1984.

29. S Banerjee and A Macdonald, 'Mental disorder in an elderly home care population: associations with health and social service use', *British Journal of Psychiatry*, Vol. 168, pp750–6, 1996.

30. K Morgan, H Dalloso, T Arie et al, 'Mental health and psychological wellbeing among the old and very old living at home', *British Journal of Psychiatry*, Vol. 150, pp808-14, 1987.

31. J Copeland, B Gurland, M Dewey et al, 'The range of mental illness among the elderly in the community: prevalence in Liverpool using the GMS-AGECAT package', *British Journal of Psychiatry*, Vol. 150, pp815–23, 1987.

32. J Lindesay, K Briggs and E Murphy, 'The Guy's/Age Concern survey: prevalence rates of cognitive impairment, depression and anxiety in an urban elderly community', *British Journal of Psychiatry*, Vol. 6, pp727–36, 1989.

33.   G Livingston, A Hawkins, N Graham et al, 'The Gospel Oak study: prevalence rates of dementia, depression and activity limitation among elderly residents in inner London', *Psychological Medicine*, Vol. 20, pp137–46, 1990.

34.   H Meltzer, B Gill and M Pettigrew, *OPCS surveys of psychiatric morbidity in Great Britain: the prevalence of psychiatric morbidity among adults aged 16-64, living in private households in Great Britain*, OPCS, 1994.

35.   S Kelly and J Bunting, 'Trends in suicide in England and Wales 1982-1996', *Population Trends*, Vol. 92, 1998.

36.   S Iliffe, S SeeTai, A Haines et al, 'Assessment of elderly people in general practice 4. Depression, functional ability and contact with services', *British Journal of General Practice*, pp371–4, 1993.

37.   M O'Hara, F Kohort and R Wallace, 'Depression among the rural elderly: a study of prevalence and correlates', *Journal of Nervous and Mental Disorders*, Vol. 173, pp582–9, 1985.

38.   E Levin, J Moriarty and P Gorbach, *Better for the Break*, HMSO, 1994.

39.   G Brown, 'Life events and social support: possibilities for primary prevention', in R Jenkins, J Newton and R Young (eds), *The Prevention of Depression and Anxiety*, HMSO, 1992.

40.   S Banerjee and A Macdonald, 'Mental disorder in an elderly home care population: associations with health and social service use', *British Journal of Psychiatry*, Vol. 168, pp750–6, 1996.

41.   J Copeland, I Davidson, M Dewey et al, 'Alzheimer's Disease, other dementias, depression and pseudo-dementia: prevalence, incidence and three year outcome in Liverpool', *British Journal of Psychiatry*, Vol. 161, pp230–9, 1992.

42.   S Banerjee, K Shamash, A Macdonald and A Mann, 'Randomised controlled trial of effect of intervention by psychogeriatric team on depression in frail elderly people at home', *British Medical Journal*, Vol. 313, pp1058–61, 1996.

43.   N Trieman and N Wills, 'The psychogeriatric population: in transition from hospital to community based services', in J Leff (ed), *Care in the Community: Illusion or Reality*, John Wiley, Chichester, 1996.

44.   M McCracken, M Boneham, J Copeland et al, 'Prevalence of dementia and depression among elderly people in black and ethnic minorities', *British Journal of Psychiatry*, Vol. 171, pp269–73, 1997.

45.   E Silveira and S Ebrahim, 'Mental health and the status of elderly Bengalis and Somalis in London', *Age and Ageing*, Vol. 24, pp474–80, 1995.

46. J Brownlie, *A Hidden Problem? Dementia Amongst Minority Ethnic Groups*, Dementia Services Development Centre, University of Stirling, 1991.

47. C Cox and A Monk, 'Minority care givers of dementia victims: a comparison of black and Hispanic families', *Journal of Applied Gerontology*, Vol. 9, pp340–55, 1990.

48. L Barclay, A Zemcov, J Blass and J Sansone, 'Survival in Alzheimer's Disease and vascular dementia' *Neurology*, Vol. 35, pp834–40, 1985.

49. T Kitwood, *Dementia Reconsidered: The Person Comes First*, Open University Press, Buckingham, 1997.

50. B Coope, C Ballard, K Saad et al, 'The prevalence of depression in the carers of dementia sufferers', *British Journal of Psychiatry*, Vol. 10, pp237–42, 1995.

51. D O'Connor, P Pollitt, M Roth et al, 'Problems reported by relatives in a community study of dementia', *British Journal of Psychiatry*, Vol. 156, pp835–41, 1990.

52. G Mountain and M Godfrey, *Respite Care Provision for Older People with Dementia: a Review of the Literature*, Nuffield Institute for Health, University of Leeds, 1995.

53. N Chappell and M Penning, 'Behavioural problems and distress among care givers of people with dementia', *Ageing and Society*, Vol. 16, pp57–73, 1996.

54. J Twigg (ed), *Carers: Research and Practice*, HMSO, 1992.

55. D Melzer, S Bedford, T Dening et al, 'Carers and the monitoring of psychogeriatric community teams', *International Journal of Geriatric Psychiatry*, Vol. 11, pp1057–61, 1996.

56. E Levin, *Carers: Problems, Strains and Services*, Oxford University Press, Oxford, 1997.

57. Audit Commission, *Finding a Place*, HMSO, 1994.

58. T Arie and D Jolley, 'Making services work: organisation and style of psychogeriatric services', in R Levy and F Post (eds), *The Psychiatry of Late Life*, Blackwell, Oxford, 1982.

59. S Kavanagh, J Schneider, M Knapp, J Beecham and A Netten, 'Elderly people with cognitive impairment: costing possible changes in the balance of care', *Health and Social Care*, Vol. 1, pp69–80, 1993.

60. A Gray and P Fenn, 'Alzheimers's Disease: the burden of the illness in England', *Health Trends*, Vol. 25, pp31–6, 1993.

61. G Livingston, M Manela and C Katona, 'Cost of community care for older people', *British Journal of Psychiatry*, Vol. 171, pp56–69, 1997.

62. M Cullen, R Blizard, G Livingston et al, 'The Gospel Oak project 1987–1990: provision and use of community services', *Health Trends*, Vol. 25, pp142–6, 1993.

63. J Yesavage, T Brink, T Rose et al, 'Development and validation of a geriatric depression screening scale: a preliminary report', *Journal of Psychiatric Research*, Vol. 17, pp37–49, 1983.

64. S Iliffe, A Eden, M Downs and C Rae, 'The diagnosis and management of dementia in primary care: development, implementation and evaluation of a national training programme', *Ageing and Mental Health*, 1998.

65. P Trainor, *Debts of Love*, Newry and Mourne Health and Social Service Trust, Co. Down, 1997.

66. I Philp and J Young, 'Audit of support given to lay carers of the demented elderly by a primary care team', *Journal of the Royal College of General Practitioners*, April 1988.

67. E Colerick and L George, 'Predictors of institutionalisation among care givers of patients with Alzheimer's Disease', *Journal of the American Geriatric Society*, Vol. 34, pp493–8, 1986.

68. Alzheimer's Disease Society, Northern Ireland, personal communication.

69. A Pattie and C Gilleard, *Manual of the Clifton Assessment Procedures for the Elderly (CAPE)*, Hodder and Stoughton, London, 1979.

70. L Schneider and P Sobin, 'Treatment for psychiatric symptoms and behavioural disturbances in dementia', in A Burns and R Levy (eds), *Dementia*, Chapman and Hall, London, 1994.

71. C Palmer, *Evidence-base Briefing: Dementia*, Gaskell, Royal College of Psychiatrists, London, 1999.

72. A Stewart, R Phillips and G Dempsey, 'Pharmacotherapy for people with Alzheimer's Disease: a Markov-cycle evaluation of five years' therapy using Donepezil', *International Journal of Geriatric Psychiatry*, Vol. 13, pp445–53, 1998.

73. Eccles et al, 'Evidence based guidelines on dementia', *British Medical Journal*, pp802–8, 1998.

74. W Rosen, R Mohr and K Davis, 'A new scale for Alzheimer's Disease', *American Journal of Psychiatry*, Vol. 141, pp1356–64, 1984.

75. P Wilkinson, 'Cognitive therapy with older people', *Age and Ageing*, Vol. 26, pp53–8, 1997.

76. M Orrell and B Woods, 'Tacrine and psychological therapies in dementia: no contest?', *International Journal of Geriatric Psychiatry*, Vol. 11, pp189–92, 1996.

77. J Kiernat, 'The use of life review activity with confused nursing home residents' *American Journal of Occupational Therapy*, Vol. 33, pp306–14, 1979.

78. T Kitwood, 'How valid is validation therapy?', *Geriatric Medicine*, April, p23, 1992.

79. R Baker, Z Dowling, L Wareing et al, 'Snoezelen: its long-term and short-term effects on older people with dementia', *British Journal of Occupational Therapy*, Vol. 60, pp213–15, May 1997.

80. E Murphy, 'With respect to old age', *British Medical Journal*, Vol. 318, pp681–2, 1999.

81. J Joffe and D Lipsey, 'Note of dissent', in Royal Commission on Long Term Care, *With Respect to Old Age*, the Stationery Office, 1999.

82. Department of Health, *L v Bournewood Community and Mental Health Trust: Decision by the House of Lords in the Appeal*, HSC 1998/122.

83. General Medical Council, *Interim Guidance. Confidentiality: Providing and Protecting Information*, British Medical Association, London, 1999.

84. I McKeith, R Perry, A Fairbairn, S Jabeen and E Perry, 'Operational criteria for senile dementia of Lewy body type', *Psychological Medicine*, Vol. 22, pp911–22, 1992.

85. T Kitwood and K Bredin, 'A new approach to the evaluation of dementia care', *Journal of Advances in Health and Nursing Care*, Vol. 1, pp41–60, 1992.

86. J Wattis and A Fairbairn, 'Towards a consensus on continuing care for older adults with psychiatric disorder', *International Journal of Psychiatry*, Vol. 11, pp163–8, 1996.

87. Royal College of Psychiatrists and Royal College of Physicians, *The Care of Older People with Mental Illness: Specialist Services and Medical Training*, Royal Colleges, 1998.

88. T Reynolds, M Orrell, G Thornicroft, M Abas, B Woods and J Hoe, 'The Camberwell assessment of need for the elderly: development, validity and reliability', *British Journal of Psychiatry*, in press 1999.

89. Nuffield Institute for Health, *Joint Investment Plans for Older People*, Nuffield Institute for Health, unpublished, 1999.

90. Social Information Systems, *A State of Confusion: A Report to the Alzheimer's Disease Society*, SIS, Knutsford, Cheshire, 1997.

Glossary

ADS	Alzheimer's Disease Society
CBT	cognitive behavioural therapy
CMHTs	community mental health teams
CPA	care programme approach
CPNs	community psychiatric nurses
ECT	electro-convulsive therapy
GDS	geriatric depression scale
GP	general practitioner
JIP	joint investment plan (health authorities and local authorities to update these annually)
MISG	mental illness specific grant
MMSE	mini mental state examination
OPCS	Office for Population Censuses and Surveys
OT	occupational therapist
PCGs	primary care groups
STG	special transitional grant (social services can spend this on residential or community care)

Index References are to paragraph numbers, Boxes and Case Studies